stop
being
mean to
yourself

stop being mean to yourself

A Story About Finding the True
Meaning of Self-Love

Melody Lynn Beattie

HarperSanFrancisco
An Imprint of HarperCollins*Publishers*

HarperSanFrancisco and the author, in association with the Basic Foundation, a not-for-profit organization whose primary mission is reforestation, will facilitate the planting of two trees for every one tree used in the manufacture of this book.

A TREE CLAUSE BOOK

HarperCollins Web Site: http://www.harpercollins.com
HarperCollins®, ☕ ®, and HarperSanFrancisco™ and A TREE CLAUSE BOOK® are trademarks of HarperCollins Publishers Inc.

FIRST EDITION

Library of Congress Cataloging-in-Publication Data
Beattie, Melody
Stop being mean to yourself: a story about finding the true meaning of self-love / Melody Beattie. —1st ed.
ISBN 0—06—251119—X (cloth)
ISBN 0—06—251120—3 (pbk.)
I. Title.
PS3552.E178S76   1997
813'.54—dc21   96—39644

97 98 99 00 01 ❖ RRDH 10 9 8 7 6 5 4 3 2 1

For my readers

Thank you for staying with me while I've grown
in my craft and in my life. As the Virginia Slims
commercial says, "We've come a long way, baby."

For Nelle, who passed during the writing of this book

Nelle, you were a fortress of courage. You fought
and won many a hard battle. Thanks for letting me
travel for you while your illness confined you to
your bed. Thanks for your time in my life.

My heart has become astir with a goodly matter.
I am saying: "My works are concerning a king."
May my tongue be the stylus of a skilled copyist.
You are indeed more handsome than the sons of
men. Charm has been poured out upon your
lips. That is why God has blessed you to time
indefinite. Gird your sword upon your thigh,
O mighty one, with your dignity and your splendor.
And in your splendor go on to success; ride in
the cause of truth and humility and righteousness,
and your right hand will instruct you in fear-
inspiring things.

Psalm 45:1–4,
NEW WORLD TRANSLATION
OF THE HOLY SCRIPTURES

Contents

Acknowledgments

This has been the most challenging book I've written in my nine-book career. I could not have done it alone. Thank God, I didn't have to—which is what I'm about to do.

I give special thanks to God, the Supreme Authority in our universe, whom I have also come to know, through the writing of this book, as Allah.

Nichole and Will, thank you both so much. Nichole, your vibrant personality and wit brought this book to life and continue to make my heart smile. Will, I am so pleased that you're becoming a part of our family. I have loved you from the first time you sat in my living room glowing with your gentle spirit and loving ways. Welcome aboard. Thank you both for staying with me through the trip and this book. You are the loves of my life. I am so proud of and pleased with both of you. A mother couldn't ask for more.

Dr. Steve Sherwin, thank you for your patience and skills and your undeviating belief in this book and me. Many of the concepts that appear in this book came from, and through, you. Thanks for everything.

Wendylee, there are not enough words to acknowledge what a trooper and copilot you've been throughout this amazingly intense, grueling, and magnificent process that began when I first (in retrospect naively) conceived the idea for this book. Thank you for your unwavering support and presence while I wandered through the Middle East. Thank you for the quality of your intuitive counsel. Thanks for the laughs. Thanks for being you and being there. I am a lucky woman to have you in my life. Who was it that said, "Everyone should have a Wendylee"? They were right. We should all be so lucky. Thanks for being my assistant, my friend, an editor, a consultant, and a spiritual and emotional touchstone.

Jhoni, thanks for being a loyal and good friend. Your well-timed telephone calls and creative inspiration guided me through some tough spots in this book. Thanks for being there for me. Thanks for bringing the spirit of L.A. into my life and this book. Thanks for your well-timed personal advice: "Melody, stop that. It's not being nice to them, it's being mean to yourself." You're brilliant, and you have a beautiful soul.

Toni, true friends are so rare in this world. Thanks for bringing friendship, color, and an appreciation for beauty into my life. It was you who called me New Year's Day and said, "I've made a resolution. I'm not going to be mean to myself anymore." Thanks for giving me the title for this book. Thanks for introducing me to Jerry, in Pasadena. Thanks for giving me a role model of what a superior woman of fine character really is.

John Steven, from the beginning we have not had a traditional mother–son relationship, but you have always been in my heart. You've fought your way through many obstacles, and you've won. I am so proud of you, and so pleased with your beautiful family—your wife, Jeannette, and my grandson, Brandon. The three of you have done an admirable job.

I must express my deep gratitude and appreciation for the people in Morocco, Algeria, and Egypt who opened their hearts and homes to me. Essam, you have a sweet, gentle spirit. Your devout love for Allah and your belief in the existence of the *special powers* continue to impress me. Thank you for all you've shown me about life. I send a special thank-you to the women of Egypt for opening your hearts to a foreigner. Fateh and Nazil, you are the heroes of Algiers. You made my time in your country memorable. "Thank you" doesn't seem adequate.

Finally, Shane Anthony, thank you so much. I wanted to leave you a great legacy. Instead, you left me one. One of the many gifts you gave me was your tremendous spirit of adventure. It was that spirit that gave me the courage to take the trip to the Middle East, to ride by the terrorist hills with little fear, and to ride that donkey down the streets of the village of Giza. Remember that night on the island, when you grabbed my hand and said, "Let's go." "Where?" I said. "For an adventure," you replied. That was six years ago. Well, you're still taking my hand and saying, "Let's go." I can't think of a better guardian angel any mom could ever have.

A Note to the Reader

I based this book in part on a trip I took through the Middle East in early 1996. It is about an initiation, a gateway I went through. It is about a gateway many of us are passing through as we approach and enter the millennium.

It could be labeled another self-help book, but it isn't a book of labels. We don't need any more. We've got too many of them. They're too convenient. They let us talk without thinking. They let us give advice without compassion. They make criticism and judgment too easy in a world where criticism and judgment come easily enough. It's not a book about pointing a finger at anyone and saying, "You're doing it wrong."

This is a book about learning to be kinder. It's about learning to be kinder to the world and people around us, as much as possible. Most importantly, it is a book about learning the art of being kinder to ourselves. It's a book about learning to love ourselves at the deepest levels, at levels perhaps deeper than anyone has trained or encouraged us to love ourselves before. It's about examining the different ways we torture, punish, abuse, and torment ourselves—and in the process of uncovering that, perhaps discovering some of the ways we torment those we love. *Stop Being Mean to Yourself* is a book about learning the art of living and loving, and the art of learning to live joyfully in a world where many of us wonder if that's possible.

I wrote it for people struggling and tired of it, people who have tried everything they know to heal themselves and their lives and who still wonder, in the wee hours of the night, if they should talk to their doctor about going on Prozac. It's for people already on antidepressants. It's for people who wonder if they can trust what they've learned, where they've been, or where they're going; people who have read all the books about the wonders of the upcoming millennium and still find themselves dealing with the reality of today; people who consistently quote the first paragraph from M. Scott Peck's book *The Road Less Traveled* where he says "life is difficult" because that's what they remember most. It's for people tired of jargon; people tired of working so hard on themselves only to find themselves staying essentially the same except for minor changes in circumstance and occasional revelations they would have had anyway; people who no longer believe the grass is greener on the other side, but even that thought doesn't console them because the idea that many people are miserable is perhaps even more frightening than the idea that they've been singled out. It's for people who have studied past lives, been to psychics, attended all the workshops, regularly visited their therapists, and still don't get what it's all about; people who know how to deal with their feelings and wonder if that overwhelming process will ever end; people who have given control of their lives, or a part of it, to others only to find themselves repeatedly disappointed when they discovered the people they turned to knew less than they did. It's for people who have glimpses that something revolutionary, spiritual, and transformational is going on, but aren't quite sure what that is.

I wrote this book for young people, middle-aged people, baby boomers, and older people.

I wrote this book for myself.

In 1986 I wrote a book entitled *Codependent No More*. In some ways, *Stop Being Mean to Yourself* is a follow-up or completion book to that one, kind of a *Codependent No More Some More*. It's a spiritual warrior's guide, a handbook for the millennium as we watch and wonder about events to come.

Come with me now to the land of Scheherazade, the fabled storyteller of the *Arabian Nights*. Let the messages you find in the pages that follow call to you on whatever level they will. I hope—no, I know, *Insha'a Allah*—you will be stirred, summoned to an adventure in your life the way I was by the mysterious, loving, enrapturing power of a crescent moon and star illuminating the sky one quiet Christmas night.

Melody

stop
being
mean to
yourself

chapter 1

The
Interrogation

Hurry," I told the taxi driver as we wound our way through the village of Giza.

He turned around to look at me. "Hurry?" he said, imitating the word with an Arabic accent. Obviously he didn't understand.

"Yes, hurry. Fast," I said, making a quick, sweeping gesture with my hand.

"Oh." He nodded in recognition. "Quickly!"

"Yes, quickly."

It had been a strange experience, spending the last three weeks in countries where few people spoke English and my best French was a *"Bon soir, Pierre"* that sounded as if I was parroting a cheap learn-to-speak-French tape. I turned around for a final look at the pyramids. Lit for the night shows, they glowed mystically on the desert skyline. I sank down into the seat and closed my eyes. Now, my driver was dutifully *hurrying.* I couldn't look. Cairo is a city with sixteen million people crammed into an area that would house a quarter of a million people in the United States. Riding in a car there is comparable to driving the 405 freeway in Los Angeles with no marked lanes and no highway patrol officers with quotas.

Many events and situations no longer surprise us, but we still don't become used to them. That's how I felt about the driving in the Middle East. It no longer surprised me, but I wasn't *used to it.* I felt relieved when we pulled into the parking lot at the Cairo Airport. I was a step closer to home. Just as I had felt convinced I was to come on this trip, despite the State Department's travel advisory warning against it, I was now equally convinced it was time to leave. I had felt almost panicky as I checked out of my hotel, then hailed a cab to the village of Giza to say good-bye to Essam before heading for the airport.

I had planned to stay here for several more weeks. I could tell Essam felt disappointed that I was leaving so soon. But he had respected my decision to leave, voicing no objections and asking only a few questions. Upon my arrival in Cairo, he had taught me the meaning of the Arabic phrase "*Insha'a Allah.*"

He explained it to me one evening when I told his sister and aunt good-bye and they said they felt sad-dened to see me leave.

"Don't worry," I said. "I will be back soon. I promise."

"Don't say that," Essam corrected me. "Never say 'I will do this.' Instead say, 'I will do this Insha'a Allah.'"

"What does that mean?" I asked.

"If God wills it," he said.

My time in the Middle East had been a dream va-cation—well, more like a codependent's dream vaca-tion. But the same vortex that had propelled me here had taken me each place I needed to go to research this book. By now, researching the book had come to mean researching a part of me and my life that needed to heal. There were times it felt more like an initiation than research.

It's a strange thing when we're in the middle of a vortex. Outside a vortex, we watch and judge. Sometimes we don't even see or feel it. But the closer we get, the more we're drawn into it. Its power begins pulling on us as we get closer and closer. Then we're sucked into the middle of the experience with a chaotic rush of emotions until at the very center we find pure, absolute peace—although if we're conscious, we know we're in a vortex. We know we're in the midst of something, learning something. Then, suddenly, it's time to leave. The energy weakens. We begin to get thrust out—pushed out—but it's still necessary to pass through the whirling centrifugal force. Sometimes it spits us out; sometimes we extricate ourselves. But it's always a centrifugal, almost magnetic, push and pull. It's vortex energy. It's the way the forces of the universe work lately—Dorothy showed us this a long time ago in *The Wizard of Oz*.

Vortexes don't just destroy, the way tornadoes sometimes do. Vortexes don't just suck us down under, like eddies in the sea. They heal, energize, teach, empower, cleanse, enlighten, and transpose. They lift us up and set us down in a new place. They bring new energy in. They discharge the old. We're never the same again after a vortex experience.

That's the way this trip had been. Each place the vortex had set me down—from the museums in Paris, to the *casbah* in Rabat, to the terrorist-infested hills of Algiers—had held a lesson, an important one. Each experience I'd been through had brought me closer to the missing piece I was searching for: stumbling, my thigh-high stockings bunched around my ankles, through the crowded Cairo *souk* at two in the morning; riding a donkey through the village of Giza; galloping on horseback across the desert to meditate inside a pyramid.

And just as elephants tummy-rumble, calling to each other about the mysteries of life, the people I met and learned from had called to me—Fateh and Nazil in Algiers, the women "locked in the box" in Cairo, and my new friend, Essam.

But now the vortex was spitting me out. It was time to go.

As we made our way to the airport, a quiet thought haunted me. *It's not over yet.* I ignored it. I wanted out; I wanted to go home.

I reached the entrance to the airport. At the Cairo terminal, the first security check is at the door. I put my luggage on the conveyor belt and walked into the building. Three young men scurried to pull my suitcases off the belt. I thanked them. Each young man then stood with his hand out, waiting for a gratuity. I shoved a few Egyptian pounds in each palm, loaded my luggage on a cart, and started pushing the cart across the terminal. A fourth man rushed up to me.

"Me too," he said, grabbing money out of my pocket.

"Stop that. You're disgusting," I screamed under my breath, the way we scream when we're out in public and we don't want anyone to know we're screaming. "You didn't even touch my luggage. Now get away."

I relaxed when I reached the next security check a few moments later. I had originally planned to fly to Greece, then fly home from there. Because of my sudden change in plans, I had rerouted through Tel Aviv. My flight to Tel Aviv didn't leave for half an hour; the line ahead moved quickly. I relaxed. I was on my way.

Suddenly a man and a young woman with long dark hair and piercing eyes, probably in her late twenties, appeared by my side. They both wore uniforms.

"Come with us, please," the dark-haired woman said.

They led me to a table in an area of the room removed from the hubbub of the terminal. They placed my suitcases on the table. The man stepped back. The woman did all the talking.

It began slowly, then built in intensity. "Why are you flying to Tel Aviv? Did you know the plane had been delayed? Why did you change your plans?"

The woman looked similar to someone you might see working as a receptionist or walking around a college campus. But she didn't act that way. She looked right through me into some space behind me that only she could see. Each question led to the next. Her vacant look and lack of emotions—either in her questions or to my responses—felt like a passive disguise for trained savagery.

To each of my responses, she replied simply, "I see." She did with words what most people can only do with knives or guns. She's good, I thought. Real good. I could have learned a few things from her about ferreting out the truth from people, especially those years I'd been married to an alcoholic. The man didn't speak to me, but occasionally she would turn to him and they'd discuss something in a language I couldn't understand. Once, I tried to turn the conversation around.

"It feels good to talk to someone so fluent in English," I said. "You speak the language well. Have you lived in America?" She replied quickly, without emotion or explanation, that she had spent time in Canada, then she resumed her questioning.

"It says on your tickets that you purchased them shortly before your departure from the United States. Why would you decide to take a trip of this magnitude on such short notice?" the woman asked. "Why would you travel alone to all the places you did? What were you doing in these countries?"

I didn't completely understand the maelstrom that had whirled me across this subterranean land. I didn't understand what was happening to me right now. But I began to unravel the mystery for her as best I could.

chapter 2

The Crescent Moon and Star

I opened the curtains in my hotel room and stared out the window at the strange combination of soot-covered modern high-rises and old Arabic shops that make up the Casablanca skyline. The noise from radios, honking cars, and ship horns created an irritating cacophonous symphony. Women hidden under veils and dark-eyed men crammed the narrow sidewalks, rushing, hurrying somewhere.

It was the beginning of my trip. I was in the heart of the city overlooking the harbor on the Atlantic coastline. Casablanca is the largest port in Morocco, the economic capital of the country, and the fourth largest city in the Arab world. Romantic illusions had filled my head about the exotic beauty I would find here. I had imagined scenery such as that pictured in travel books—stone structures with pottery, foliage, and the use of vibrant colors so reminiscent of this part of the world.

Casablanca had all the colors I had anticipated. An exotic combination of tangerine, red, gold, blue, and green decorated my hotel room. But Casablanca was not what I had expected. Poverty bordering on desperation permeated most of this seaport city—including this four-star hotel. The vibrations emanating from this place were so foreign, so exotic, so dense my body could barely adjust.

I had flown into Casablanca from Paris the night before last. It was dark when I arrived. On the way in from the airport, I noticed that drivers didn't bother using headlights at night, except momentarily when they approached an oncoming car. It saved on batteries.

Paris had been everything I always imagined it would be—from all the stories I heard about my

French ancestry, from my years studying French in high school, and from all the times I had seen the Eiffel Tower in magazines and movies.

I chose what I thought would be a fine hotel for my stay in Paris. But when the manager opened the door to my room, I felt instantly overwhelmed. The room looked so formal, so beautiful, so elegant and refined. So French. It was like a palace. The room was stuffed with Louis XV antiques. An oil painting framed in gold hung prominently over the bed. All the furnishings in the room were edged in gold. I just stood and stared, my mouth agape.

"C'est bien?" the manager asked.

I had no idea what he was talking about—none whatsoever. I tried to retrieve some kind of memory from a French class of thirty years ago, but I couldn't.

I spent most of my first day in France in my room resting up from the trip from the United States, adjusting to the time change, and feeling intimidated by the luxury. Then, I grabbed some magazines and studied the attractions. I was flying out of Paris the following day, but I was determined to see a few sights before I left.

On my way to the airport for my flight to Casablanca, I did a whirlwind tour. I sat on a stone ledge at a scenic overlook and stared out through the winter fog *at the Eiffel Tower. I strolled through the Museum of Man, a special historical exhibit. This museum is divided into sections that represent the various countries in Africa—the continent where many anthropologists believe human life originated on this planet. Each country's display depicts scenes about the same issues people have struggled with since the beginning of time: birth, health, marriage, family, religion, divination, and death. Then, on my way to the airport, I raced through the Louvre, briefly connecting with some of most breathtaking art in the world as the vortex funneled me deeper into the heart of this tour.*

I had chosen Paris because I wanted to get off to a good start, one with a little flair and comfort, as I had expected my time in the Middle East to be stressful and probably deprived of comfort. Now, staring out the window in my room in Casablanca, it looked as if I had been right. I wasn't looking for comfort here, anyway. I was looking for something else.

I planned to spend a few days here in Casablanca. I would store my luggage at this hotel, then fly into Algeria tomorrow, carrying only a backpack. I would stay in Algeria for a few days, maybe a week. I wouldn't decide for certain until I arrived there and saw what was happening. Then I would fly back here, get my luggage, and go on to Cairo. From there, I thought possibly I would fly to Greece. Other than for the final leg of the trip in Greece, I had made hotel arrangements for at least the first night in each city I planned to visit. I wanted to be flexible and let the rhythm of each country and the rhythm of the story that unfolded guide my plans.

I closed the curtains and rode the elevator downstairs to the hotel lobby. Outside the combination restaurant and bar, a Humphrey Bogart look-alike smiled and nodded to welcome me, his head bobbing like a human puppet. I went in, sat down at the bar, and ordered a café au lait.

I looked around the room. There were two other people—including the bartender—besides me. The bartender wore a navy blue, short-waisted suit that resembled a military uniform. A chic woman with short black hair and wearing high platform shoes sat in a booth to my left. She looked as if she was in her late twenties, maybe from Italy. She kept glancing toward the doorway. I assumed she was waiting for someone.

When the bartender brought my coffee, I looked at the milk, hesitating for just a moment. I wanted to be careful about what I ate and drank on this trip.

Hell, I was careful at home. But they boiled the water for coffee. This should be fine. I poured the warm milk into the demitasse of espresso.

"It's quiet here," I said to the bartender.

"It's Ramadan," he said.

Although I had heard about Ramadan, I had not been aware it would be taking place during my travels. Ramadan is a month of fasting in Islamic countries, the month when Muslims believe God—or Allah—sent the Koran down to Mohammed, the prophet and founder of the Islamic faith. Islamic religion prohibits Muslims from eating, drinking, smoking, and sexual activity during daylight hours— from dawn to dusk—during Ramadan. Ramadan ends when a reliable source sights the new moon. Muslims consider this a time not so much of deprivation, but of obedience to God.

"Where are you from?" the bartender asked.

I told him I was from the United States, feeling complimented by his question. I had wanted to blend in, to not stand out as an American tourist traipsing through the Middle East. To do that, my friend and hairdresser, Angelo, had cut my hair to less than two inches long, then colored it almost pitch-black. I had carefully chosen dark, inconspicuous clothing for this trip.

"Business or pleasure?" the bartender asked.

"Business," I said. "I'm a writer."

"What brings you *here?*" he asked.

"A story," I said. "But it didn't really bring me *here*. I'm just in Morocco to get my bearings and find a place to store my luggage. Tomorrow, I'm flying into Algiers."

Wrong answer, I thought, seeing the scowl on his face. I was used to that look by now. I provoked it whenever I told someone I was going to Algeria. I had seen that look on Christmas Day, back home in Los Angeles, when I had told my friend Maurice, a Moroccan Frenchman who lives in the United States, that I was going to Algiers. The scowling disapproval no longer bothered me. I hadn't let it stop me when I planned this trip. I certainly wasn't going to let it stop me now. I dug out a handful of *dirhams*, the Moroccan currency, paid for my coffee, walked outside, and hailed a cab.

"Take me to the *souk*, please," I said to the driver.

"The *souk?*" the driver asked, looking at me like I was crazy.

"Yes. The *souk*," I said.

I had heard about *souks* before my trip began. They were huge marketplaces, cities within a city, old Arab towns tucked away in the midst of urban high-rises. I heard that some people spent their whole lives in *souks*. They were born, lived, and died in there. One travel agent said people can go in and never be seen again. I had also heard stories about the wonderful open-air herb markets in the *souks*, the clothing, food, and silver goods. I wanted to see for myself.

The driver parked the car at an intersection where the streets began to narrow to one lane.

"We're here," he said.

"Wait for me," I instructed him. "I'll be back in an hour."

He smiled as if he knew something I didn't.

I lasted five minutes. I had walked only two blocks when three men, probably in their early twenties, began first following, then closing in on me. I hurriedly crossed the street and ran back to the cab, making my way through the shoving people, the bicyclists, and the old wooden carts.

"I'm done here," I said. "Take me back to the hotel, please."

I returned to my room and began rearranging my luggage, preparing for tomorrow's flight to Algiers. I had traveled a lot, both in the United States and around the world. Sometimes I had gone for pleasure. Mostly, it was for business. In 1989, during one of the controversies in Central America, I had gone to Honduras with some other media personnel from Minnesota. It was part of my work as a journalist for the daily paper in the town where I lived. We had flown to Panama and Honduras in an Air Force bomber. A five-star general had given us a tour. We were kept under armed guard in a hotel. Then we were flown into the heart of Honduras in a helicopter.

I was *used to* going out and finding the story.

Only this time, I was going alone.

I brought my suitcases down to the hotel lobby and asked the concierge to secure my luggage for a few days. I thanked him, tucked my claim checks in my purse, and returned to my room. It didn't look as if much was going to happen here. This city wasn't opening up for me. I guess I hadn't expected it to. I had only intended this to be a safe place to store my luggage while I flew into the not-so-safe neighboring country of Algeria.

As the sun set, the chanting from the evening prayers rose from the mosques scattered throughout the city, filling the air like verbal incense. Lightning flashed, thunder crackled, and the sound of the howling winds intermingled with the prayers and songs. Then the winds began to blow so hard the windows rattled and shook.

I remembered the first time the winds had blown, the winds of the vortex that brought me here. It was the night after Thanksgiving. They're strange winds, the Santa Anas. They blow hard, yet warm. They're different from any wind I've ever felt.

The next day, I discovered the Santa Anas had blown so hard they whisked my garbage can away. While I stood on the street behind my house looking for my trash can, my daughter, Nichole, pulled into the driveway with her boyfriend, Will.

I like Will. He's an actor in Los Angeles. He's young, but he's had a degree of success already. He has a good spirit and a good heart. I liked him from the first time Nichole brought him home and introduced him to me.

That day, Nichole and Will were glowing when they got out of the car. They had something important to tell me.

"We had a great experience last night," Nichole said. "We thought we were going to Venice to have dinner with some friends of a friend. It turned out to be more than that, though. Master Huang was there. He's a special holy man from Taiwan. He only comes to the United States once or twice a year. He pulled Will and me aside, talked to us for a while, and asked us if we wanted to receive our Tao. We said yes. So we went

through this beautiful ceremony and got our Tao. We also got the Three Treasures, the three secrets to life. But I can't tell you about those. We promised not to."

Nichole tried to explain more about this mysterious ceremony and exactly what it meant, but I didn't understand.

"Mostly, getting your Tao means that your karma has ended," Nichole said. "We don't have to reincarnate or recycle again, evermore."

I have never understood karma. I don't know—not in the way a journalist needs to know—whether reincarnation exists or not. Sometimes I think if we care so much about recycling cans, God would probably want to recycle souls. As for karma, whatever it is and whatever it means, it has always sounded like trouble to me. And I certainly wished I could get mine to end.

I glanced up and down the road one more time, as if staring hard enough could bring that garbage can back. Then I gave up and headed down the stairway leading to the house.

"Tell me the secrets," I said to Nichole.

She refused.

"I'm your mother," I said firmly.

She refused.

"Are they like . . ."

"Let it go, Mom," she said. "I'm not telling."

I didn't think about the vortex, the Three Treasures, Master Huang, karma, or my trash can again for a while.

As the end of the year approached, I was busy with the holidays and my travel preparations. I wasn't excited—not the way we feel when we're going on a vacation. I knew then this trip was going to be intense. My plan was to research my next book, but I knew from the start it was about more than research. The trip was an important part of my life. It was something I had to do.

When I saw that crescent moon and star in the sky on Christmas night, I knew for sure I had to go. The newspaper, the radio, all the guests who had come to my house for Christmas Day were buzzing about this crescent moon and star in the sky. The newspaper was calling it a phenomenon—"Venus Kissing the Moon." I didn't know about all that; I only knew how I felt when I stood outside and looked up at that beautiful sliver of moon with the glowing star at its tip.

It had been only the night before, Christmas Eve, that I had told Nichole the Christmas story. We were driving into Santa Monica to do some last-minute shopping. She wanted to get a book for Will, and one or two other small gifts. We both felt a little dispirited.

Holidays had been difficult in our family since my son, Shane, died. This holiday season was no exception.

While "Deck the Halls" blared on the radio, a dull throbbing pain pounded in each of us. This was our fifth Christmas since Shane's death. This holiday pain didn't surprise us anymore, but we still weren't used to it. I wanted to cheer up Nichole; I wanted us both to find some meaning, even in the pain. So I just started talking while we drove down the Pacific Coast Highway.

"You know, everyone talks about the Christmas story, and they talk about no room in the inn, and they talk about all the events that took place that day," I said. "But some other things happened, too, that were an important part of that story. Do you know that three men—we call them wise men, or Magi—looked up in the sky and they saw a star? They had enough faith in themselves, in their hearts, in God, and in the universe to start out on a journey across the land to be part of something that they couldn't see, couldn't know, couldn't touch—couldn't even read about. They just had a feeling, a sense. They knew how connected they were to the universe. They knew that star meant something and it meant something important. They knew how connected God was to the universe, to the world around them. So they started their journey to Bethlehem—a trip that took months, maybe years, across the desert.

"Yes, the day Jesus was born is important. So is the message of having faith and of honoring our connection

to the universe and how it speaks to us. So is the story of the wise men, and how they must have felt, and what it took for them to make that trip. That's a Christmas story, too," I finished quietly.

Many subtle incidents and events had led to this trip and propelled me into it. I had known for years—in that quiet way we know things—that I would someday be journeying into Africa, although I hadn't known exactly when or where. As the time for this trip drew closer, my sense of knowing the right time and place became clearer.

Last year, to research a meditation book I was working on, I had loaded my computer in my Jeep and traveled for several months around the United States. That trip had been research for that book and a test to see if the universe would dance with me and tell me the story I was trying to write and learn.

It did. And that trip prepared me for this trip.

Now I was here as a journalist, a storyteller, *and* a student. I was about to test my skills in the Middle East.

In looking back, I think my whole life led up to this trip—or at least the last ten years. It was as if I had been searching for a missing piece. I had been searching for it since I wrote *Codependent No More*. No matter what I did or tried, I couldn't find it. I suspected this trip would hold the key to that missing piece.

Then, on New Year's Eve, when the winds of that old vortex blew again, I knew for sure this trip would lead me to what I was looking for.

That night, I went to a party for a while. I wasn't feeling too social, so I left the party early. By then, the winds were blowing so hard I could barely stand erect as I walked to my car.

I went home and wrote a list of all my resentments, fears, betrayals, and dead dreams. I tossed the pages in the fireplace and set them on fire. I sat cross-legged on the floor and watched my list turn to ashes.

Moments later, all the lights in the house blacked out. Then the winds blew so hard that the windows rattled and the house shook and my bird, Max, fell off her perch. I opened her cage door and let her jump on my shoulder. I found a flashlight, turned it on, and set it on the table. We just sat there—my bird and I—in the middle of that floor, listening to the winds shake the house.

The next morning, when I went outside, my trash can was gone. The winds had blown it away again.

What I didn't fully understand, or understand at all, was that on November 25, 1995, the time when the winds had blown before, a group of people had assembled in a back room of a small house in Venice, California. The house is only a couple blocks from the pounding Pacific Coast and the famous Venice boardwalk. While roller skaters skated by the open-air shops, carefully avoiding the eyes of the deranged beggars, Master Huang ceremoniously awarded the Tao to the twelve people sitting on metal folding chairs in the back room.

First the men, then the women, were called by name to come to the front of the room. Each person knelt according to the place the Chinese woman assisting Master Huang indicated. The altar glowed with candles. A girl of about nineteen tenuously took a position in the back row of the women kneeling before the altar. The Chinese woman motioned for the girl to trade places and take the honored position in front of the incense pot. The girl held the incense and placed it, at the appropriate time, in the container, as she had been instructed to do.

Master Huang recited a series of liturgies in Chinese. Stumbling over the words, the participants repeated these sacred Chinese phrases. Master Huang then told the participants that their names were now officially recorded in the Book of Life and that they had just received their Tao. He went on to say that just as the candles on the altar burned brightly, so did the light within each of them. Those people who had

*received their Tao, including the nineteen-year-old
girl, returned to their chairs.*

*Carefully, so as to be understood with his Chinese
accent, Master Huang then gave each participant the
Three Treasures. He traced the Three Treasures to
their biblical origins. Then everyone in the room took
a vow of secrecy concerning these Treasures.*

*Before the ceremony ended, Master Huang told
each participant that he or she had now received the
keys to the Kingdom of Heaven—in the afterlife and in
this world. Their karma had ended. Reincarnation
would cease. They had reached and achieved the state
the ancients called enlightenment.*

It was a sign of the times, a gift of the times.

Now, lying on my bed in the hotel room in Casablanca listening to the prayers of Ramadan mixed
with the howling winds, I knew I had chosen to be
here—in the Middle East—at a spiritually powerful
time. This wasn't an accident. It was time for me to
remember, and trust, why I was here.

When my friend Angelo had cut my hair, he had
called this excursion "an adventure." But it wasn't a
dare-devil trip. It was more than that.

Sometimes in life, we feel led to do things that
don't seem rational. This trip was one of those
things. People had scowled and said they could not

understand why I would want to go to the places I was going. There had been times it sounded crazy to me, too. But I had scrutinized my motives and talked to a few trusted people, who agreed. Although it appeared crazy, it wasn't. I was willing to do anything and go anywhere to find the story—the story for this book and for my life. And I knew I could find that story in the Middle East.

This trip was a leap of faith.

THIS WAS A BUSINESS TRIP. This was a personal trip. But this was a destiny trip, too," I said to the woman interrogating me in the airport in Cairo. "I had all sorts of illusions about this trip. I had dreams about traveling to the deepest parts of Africa, on safari. Maybe I'd learn something from the Pygmy tribes, some magical secrets to life. Or maybe I'd have a grand revelation in the pyramids about the mystery of life after death."

"Is that what happened?" the woman asked, her eyes penetrating my soul.

"What I learned about," I said, "was the mystery of life *before* death."

chapter 3

Gunfire

Just as people report hearing a sound like the rumbling of a freight train before a tornado passes by, I heard the rumblings of the vortex that picked me up from my home in southern California and carried me across the northern rim of the African continent long before it hit. I knew for years that I would someday venture into Africa. But I didn't know it would be Algeria until the month before I left.

"Go to France. Go to Italy. Go to Greece. But don't go to Algeria," my friend Maurice had warned me on Christmas night when he learned of my plans.

His warning wasn't news. I had read the travel advisory issued by the United States government. Terrorist activities were rampant. A number of foreigners had been kidnapped and killed in recent years. Traveling there was not advised, and Americans who chose to be there anyway were instructed to have armed protection. I would be a woman traveling alone, with no guns or bodyguard. Yet I was drawn there. I knew I had to go. I also knew I'd be safe. I couldn't explain this to Maurice. I didn't try.

"I'm not kidding, Melody," Maurice had repeated. "It's dangerous. You could be killed. They're in the midst of a civil war."

"Maurice, don't fuss. I'll be fine," I had said. "I've lived most of my life in the midst of a civil war—mine against myself . . ."

Now, in Casablanca, I checked out of my hotel room, hailed a cab, and headed for the airport to catch my flight to Algiers. It was 6:00 A.M. The cab was dirty. It stunk. The upholstery on the seat was ripped to shreds. The cab driver looked as if he had slept all night in his car.

"You won't like Casablanca," my friend Maurice had said. "It's a dirty seaport city."

Maurice had been right about Casablanca. For just a moment, as I boarded the airplane, I wondered if he was right about Algeria, too.

A few months before this trip, I had visited an old Chinese healer in Pasadena, a gentle Buddhist monk who used few words. He worked on my energy, my *chi*, for a while. "You're moving to a new level," he said. "That's all you need to know for now. Go through the motions of taking care of yourself. Sit with the pain, and all your emotions, the best that you can. Do your daily disciplines. And be gentle with yourself."

Video games, the kind that come with a computer, often have different levels of play: beginner, intermediate, and master. When you move to a new level of play, it doesn't get easier. It becomes more of a challenge. The playing field is larger. The action is faster and more complicated.

In Aikido, or any other martial art, there are many different levels, or *dans,* of skill. Each time a student moves to the next level, he or she has to pass a test. And when the student reaches that new level, it's not easier. He or she is required to use all the skills acquired so far, plus learn new ones. The new level is more complicated, more difficult, and more of a challenge. And however accomplished, the student begins anew as a student at the new level.

The place where a martial art student practices is called a *dojo*. That means place of enlightenment. Some people say our lives are our *dojo*.

I had moved to new levels before.

Fifteen years ago, I was six years into a marriage to an alcoholic. In the process of frantically trying to do everything right, which then meant controlling everyone and everything but me, I lost myself. I disappeared. In the mush of believing lies and lying to myself, my spiritual, mental, and emotional powers waned into nonexistence. I became a vindictive, victimized, passively irate amoeba. I didn't leave the house for years, except to go to market.

That changed—or at least began to change—in one moment when I stopped pointing at everyone around me, screeching, "Look what you're doing to me," and instead began looking at myself.

In Aikido, a nonaggressive martial art I would begin studying years later, my sensei, or teacher, talked about the golden ball of power each of us has in our solar plexus—a golden ball that radiates in a wide arc around us. Although I didn't know about this golden

ball of power back then, I started to see the first glim-
mers of its light.

I spent the next five years learning the lessons at this
new level. I learned I could stop trying to control other
people and instead take responsibility for myself. I
learned I could allow others to live with the inevitable
and consequential results of their choices and destiny.
Rather than torque my head off my neck and implode
my insides obsessing, I learned I had options—letting
go, detaching, becoming peaceful. I realized I no
longer had to let others control me. Hallelujah! I was
free. Well, almost. But at least I added a little light to
that golden ball of power each day.

I added the word "no" to my vocabulary, too. I
learned I didn't have to let others lie to, abuse, or ma-
nipulate me for their own conscious—and sometimes
less-than-conscious—motives. I began to feel my emo-
tions even when others preferred I didn't. I discovered
I no longer had to stay trapped in relationships or situ-
ations that made me so wretchedly miserable. I got to
have a life, too.

Slowly, over those years, I began to live it.

Ten years ago, I moved to a new level again. I di-
vorced my husband, took my two young children—
Shane and Nichole—by the hand, and began my
family and life anew as a single parent. I jumped into

*my career and wrote a book about what I had learned
at the last level, a book called* Codependent No More.
*That's that, I thought, dusting off my hands and turn-
ing in the manuscript. I have solved that problem.*

*But to my surprise, along with this new dimension
of life came a new dimension of lessons. Some were in-
vigorating, some challenging, some confusing. And
one—the sudden death of my son in 1991 from a ski
accident—broke my heart.*

*I found out there was more life to live than I had
ever imagined. I also discovered there were deeper
places in me that needed healing, cleansing, and re-
newing—places I didn't know existed, either. Often
the old lessons, the lessons of the other levels, reappeared in different shapes and forms or wearing a
disguise. Whenever that happened, I wondered if I was
doing something wrong, and I doubted the insights I
once thought I had.*

I didn't yet understand about levels.

Now, the energy in my life had begun to shift
again. It would take months before I would really see
and believe what the Buddhist monk from Pasadena
had said. I was moving to a new level. This trip was
an initiation, a test. It would be a review of the
lessons of the past, in all their shapes and forms, and
a portent of things to come. While some of the

lessons would be obvious, many at this new level would be more subtle. Finding each one would be like solving a mystery.

The flight to Algiers was a short one, about two hours. As the plane swooped down to land at Houari Boumedienne Airport, I was struck by the pronounced natural beauty of this harbor city. Algiers, or El Djazair, was nestled in the Sahel Hills between the Sahara Desert and the Mediterranean. The sea was bluer than any water I had ever seen. The surf was gentle; waves barely feathered its smooth surface. Old French tenements and European housing dotted the hillside. The fertile landscape looked like a patchwork of green velvet.

I was nervous when we landed. I didn't know what to expect in a country torn by revolution and terrorism. I disembarked the plane, prepared for the worst. I found the airport strangely quiet and calm—different from peaceful. I immediately recognized the feeling.

I was in the eye of a vortex.

I anticipated that passing through customs would be an ordeal. It surprised me when the officers—young men in their twenties—smiled and welcomed me to their country. They were friendlier than customs officers I had encountered anywhere else in the world.

I grabbed my backpack and exchanged some currency. As I headed for the front door of the airport, intending to hail a cab, one of the young men intercepted me. He guided me into a side office and left me in the care of a young woman with shoulder-length chestnut-brown hair.

I gave her the name of the hotel where I intended to stay.

She called to verify my reservations. Then she told me to wait in her office until the hotel shuttle arrived. Half an hour later, she escorted me outside to the parking lot and the van. Other than milling pockets of armed guards, it looked like a normal airport anywhere in the world.

As we pulled onto the highway leading to downtown Algiers, I stared out the window with a mixture of curiosity and fear. The roads were almost deserted. I tensed each time we passed a barricade, remembering the travel advisory issued by the U.S. Department of State: "Danger to foreigners is extremely high. Substantial armed protection is recommended. Airline terminals and ports are particular targets of terrorist activity. Avoid regularly scheduled commercial flights. There is a terrorist campaign being waged against foreigners. Daily violence since 1994. Over 100 kidnappings of foreigners. Adequate protection is not possible. Roadblocks are common, as well as false roadblocks set up by terrorists as ambushes. No overland travel recommended. Terrorists threaten to kill all foreigners who will not leave the country."

I didn't know about the seriousness of the unrest when I first decided to come to Algeria. The travel advisory had concerned Wendy, who works with me in the United States. It had worried me, too. I had considered rearranging my plans. But when I discussed my plans and the potential problems in Algeria with my daughter, Nichole, she felt the same way I did—if I trusted my instincts, I would be fine.

I hadn't encountered any problems obtaining my visa from the Algerian Embassy in Washington, D.C. They seemed glad to have me visit their country. They had not been nearly as concerned as the U.S. State Department.

When asked if it was accurate that travel in Algeria was extremely dangerous and that a number of foreigners had been killed, the male voice on the phone at the Algerian Embassy had replied, "Oh, it's not that dangerous. Yeah, people get killed, but people get killed anywhere. It's not that bad."

When we reached the hotel, uniformed guards stopped and searched the shuttle. We then passed through a barricade manned by armed guards into a cordoned-off area. I noticed that a high, barbed-wire fence surrounded the entire hotel. The shuttle dropped me off. Crossing the walkway to the hotel entrance was like crossing a moat into a fort.

A man in a uniform searched me again when I entered the hotel. As I walked to the reception desk, I looked up and around. The hotel was new, modern. I could see all the way up to the tenth floor from where I stood in the foyer. But something was missing. I filled out the registration form, gave the woman my credit card, then looked around. That's what was missing—*people*.

I scanned the area looking for the stand containing pamphlets and flyers for tourist attractions, the kind commonly seen in hotels. That was missing, too. I motioned to the woman behind the counter, an attractive dark-haired woman in her early twenties.

"I suppose there's no day tours?"

She shook her head, avoiding my eyes.

"I was hoping to look around," I said.

"I'm sorry," she said.

She turned and walked away. I took the elevator to the ninth floor, let myself into my room, and flopped down on the bed. I wasn't a guest in a hotel; I was a hostage in an almost empty fort. There was nowhere to go, and no one to meet. I looked around the room. There were no tour books, no magazines, no guides to this city. I walked to the window and opened the curtains. I could see a small speck of harbor through the tiny window. I had now traveled halfway around the world to sit in my room.

Shots rang out, shattering the air outside the hotel.

Maybe it's for the best, I thought, closing the curtains.

I called down to the front desk and scheduled a massage. When I arrived at the health club, the young woman sitting behind the desk directed me to a large room off to the side. I went in. A girl, maybe eighteen, stood in the corner.

"I'm here for my massage," I said.

She just stared at me.

"Do you speak English?" I asked.

She shook her head.

"Massage?" I said.

She just looked at me. I started making rubbing gestures at myself, to try to show her what I meant. I started rubbing up and down my arm. Then I rubbed my shoulder, and my legs.

Her eyes widened in horror.

"Massage," I said. I continued rubbing at myself, trying to establish communication. It wasn't working.

She edged around me, then began backing out of the room.

This has gone far enough, I thought. I took off my clothes and lay down on the table.

After a skittish massage, I walked around the hotel for a while, then returned to my room. I turned on the television. There weren't many choices for stations. I turned it off and started paging through an English translation of a Middle Eastern newspaper I had picked up at the airport. I read an article about the latest fatal act of terrorism here. I also read with some interest a story about governments of other countries now allowing journalists and priests to act as spies.

Hmmm, I thought.

I thumbed through the rest of the paper, then put it down. I sat on the bed for a while, then sat on the chair for a while, then went back to the bed. I looked at the walls. I looked at the furniture. Then I picked up the phone and called Wendy, back in the United States, the woman I work with.

"How's the magical mystery tour going?" she asked.

"The only drama I'm going to find here," I said, "is a grinding internal one that lies somewhere between jet lag and menopause."

By the time I hung up the phone, it was getting dark outside and cold inside. I was acutely aware of my aloneness. What was I doing here? What had I possibly been thinking of, coming here? A strong wave of self-loathing and self-contempt replaced any sense of adventure, any sense of feeling right about being here, and particularly any sense of being guided.

When I had told Nichole I was writing a book about how to stop being mean to yourself, she had just smiled. "Oh, I see," she said. "It's going to be a mystery."

Well, she was right. It was a mystery. So was this trip and what I was doing here, in one of the most tortured, perilous, hot spots on the globe. Did I really believe someone would just knock on my door and say, "Hey! I'm glad you're here. I've been waiting for you to come so I could show you around and tell you my story"?

I ordered some tea from room service, ran some hot water, and took a bath. Gunfire rang out intermittently outside the window. I put on a sweat suit, crawled under the covers, and went to bed.

I had almost dozed off when I heard a knock on my door.

That's funny, I thought. I can't imagine they'd have turn-down service. Maybe it's room service, and they want their tray back.

Go away, I thought. Let me sleep.

The rapping continued.

I got up, stumbled to the door, and looked through the peephole. A man in his middle twenties stood outside the door. He glanced nervously up and down the corridor. I latched the chain lock and opened the door a crack.

"What do you want?" I asked.

"My name is Mafateh," he whispered. "I work at the hotel, in another division. The girl at the front desk is my friend. She said you were asking for something. I think I can help."

I scanned him through the crack in the door. He wore a dark blue suit that looked like a hotel employee uniform. With his hiked-up pants and chubby cheeks, he had an Arabian boy-next-door look. His eyes were gentle. He looked frightened, but safe. I unlatched the chain, opened the door, and let him in.

I introduced myself, then stumbled over his name, trying to repeat it. He told me to call him "Fateh."

"Just like 'fatty' in your language," he said proudly.

We talked for a while. It took only moments for me to feel as if I had known Fateh for a long time.

This was the first time I had connected with anyone on this trip. I explained that I would be in Algiers for at least three days, maybe longer. I said I wanted to see the country and talk to the people, and that I needed a guide to do that—someone to drive me around.

"It's not safe to drive around," he said.

"Please," I said.

He shook his head.

"*S'il vous plait,*" I said, repeating myself in French. I was begging. I knew it. "This is probably the only time in my life I will ever be here . . ."

He looked at me, scanned my appearance, then reluctantly agreed.

"Maybe it will be all right," he said. "You look like you could be from my country. Be in the hotel lobby by 9:30 tomorrow morning. Wear dark clothes, clothing that does not look like it is from America. Do not speak to anyone. Do not tell anyone where you are going or what you are going to do."

I thanked him, stuffed some Algerian currency in his hand, and latched the door behind him as he left.

In a matter of moments, the energy of this entire trip had shifted dramatically, moved to a new level. Whatever mysterious vortex had brought me here, to this part of the world, was now going to funnel me below the surface. It was time to take a deep breath and dive in.

THE SHARP VOICE OF THE interrogator ripped me out of my story and brought me back to the airport in Cairo.

"What kind of books do you write?" she demanded.

I looked around the terminal. The hubbub had dissipated. Except for one or two travelers, the only people I could see were airport employees and the man and woman who were interrogating me.

"The eight books I've written have all been about spiritual growth and healing," I said. "They are what we call self-help books in my country. That's what I'm working on now, too."

"You say you write books about spiritual growth and healing. Yet you traveled to Algeria, a country dominated by terrorism. What could the people there possibly have to do with the subject matter you write about and the people who live in your part of the world?" she asked.

By now, I was drenched in sweat and getting very tired. I thought I had told these people more than enough, more than they wanted or needed to know. I wanted to get this over with. But I wanted to cooper- ate, too. So I carefully tried to tell the sable-haired lady with the piercing eyes what the people in Algiers had shown me.

chapter 4

Conversations with a Warrior

E ach culture, country, or city is its own vortex of energy—a swirling funnel of collective past and current beliefs, emotions, intentions, and values. Los Angeles is the vortex of the cinema and television industry. Washington, D.C., is a political vortex. At 9:30 A.M. on Saturday, January 27, 1996, I put the final touches on my makeup, fastened my money belt around my waist, and rode the elevator down to the lobby to meet Fateh. I

45

was about to go on a day tour of Algiers, the capital of Algeria and the world capital and *vortex* of terrorism.

The sixties—that tumultuous, memorable time of President John F. Kennedy, Martin Luther King, Jr., and the Vietnam War gave birth to many forms of political and personal expression. Peace movements, demonstrations, and rallies became popular forms of social protest, powerful tactics to effect change in democracies. But the sixties also gave birth to the underside—*the darker side*—of speaking out for a cause. That octopus of terror, the international terrorist network, simultaneously began to stretch its tentacles around the globe. Its members were not only willing to die for their cause; they were primed to kill for it, deliberately using cold-blooded tactics that would send shock waves of terror to the masses, making victims of them, too.

The first waves were sent around the world in 1968, when terrorists hijacked an Israeli airplane, then forced its pilot to fly to Algiers.

Over the ensuing years, the tentacles of terror reached closer and closer to home. In 1972, terrorists attacked Israeli athletes at the Munich Olympics. In 1976, we watched Israeli commandos perform their daring and brilliant rescue raid on Entebbe. In 1986, the United States bombed Algeria's neighbor, Libya, hoping to destroy its leader, Muammar al-Qaddafi. In December 1988, as Pan Am flight 103 passed over Lockerbie, Scotland, on its way from London to New York, a bomb exploded, killing 270 people. Of them, 187 were Americans.

By the early nineties, the shock waves from world terrorism had reached Stillwater, Minnesota, where I lived at the time. A rash of pipe bombings and bomb threats, coupled with the Persian Gulf War and a national FBI terrorism alert, had me and many others looking over our shoulders. One afternoon, my son, Shane, asked me to take him and a group of friends to a basketball game at a local sports arena. "No," I had said. "It's not safe. It's a target. Choose something else."

In February 1993, terrorists bombed the World Trade Center in New York City. On April 19, 1995, a bomb exploded outside the Federal Building in Oklahoma City, a structure housing a day-care center. This time 169 people were killed. Of them, 19 were children.

Over the years, as bomb threats continued to increase, the United States had responded with increased security measures. The most noticeable change occurred at airports. Travelers in the United States could no longer simply check in and board a plane. They had to show photo identification. They had to answer questions. "Did you pack your luggage? Did anyone give you anything to transport?" We as a nation began to react to terrorism with subtle antiterrorist tactics. Now I was groomed, prepped, and ready for a drive by the terrorist training camps in the foothills of Algiers—one of the places contemporary terrorism had begun.

Fateh was waiting for me in the lobby. He scanned my appearance and approved. My instincts had been right on this trip. It had been easy to follow his instructions of the night before, to dress in un-American garb. I had brought only one extra set of clothing with me. I wore a dark, loose-fitting sweater and pants. With my short dark hair and olive skin, I felt almost invisible in this cultural mix of French, Arabian, and Berber heritage.

Fateh gave me my next set of instructions as he whisked me through the security checkpoints on the way to the parking lot.

"We are going to the country today," he said. "I have arranged for my friend Nazil to come with us. He is a college graduate. He has studied English for many years and speaks the language better than I do. He can tell you things that I cannot because there are many words in your language I do not know. We have not been for a drive to the country or to the parks for a long time. It will be a fun day for all of us. But there are dangers."

Fateh stopped walking and turned to me. "Do not speak to anyone, even if you are spoken to. If anyone comes to us, if anyone stops our car—even the gendarmes—*do not speak. Do not look in their eyes. Look down at your feet and be silent.* That is the only way we will be safe," he said. "Do you understand?"

Fateh looked so intense. "Not even a quick *'Bon jour'*?" I asked, trying to lighten the mood. "I'm getting better with my French . . ."

He glared at me. "Not a word," he said. "Do not speak one word."

"I understand," I said.

I sat on the passenger side of the front seat of Fateh's old Rambler. Fateh started to get in the driver's side, but before he could the car seat collapsed, falling backwards. He groaned, sighed, then dug under the seat, pulled out a screwdriver, and began tinkering with the seat back. Fixing the car would become part of this day's routine. It was part of the daily routine for many people here. Most of the automobiles were old, used cars—the kind we call junkers in America.

While Fateh worked on the seat, I turned to the young man, Nazil, sitting in the back seat of the car.

He had dark wavy hair and graceful features. He was of slight build, much thinner than Fateh. I would later learn he was twenty-four years old—one year younger than Fateh.

I told Nazil my name was Melody and I was pleased to meet him. I offered him my hand.

"It is my pleasure to meet you," he said, "and my honor to spend the day with a woman from your country. I have studied the English language most of my life but have only been able to use it in the classroom. I am happy today to have the opportunity to use the language I have studied so hard."

After Fateh fixed the seat, he climbed in the car, shifted the gear stick, let the car roll backwards, and fired up the engine.

We drove around the narrow city streets of downtown Algiers for a while. A small number of men were out walking, some in groups, some alone. One man hurried across the street in front of us. He was carrying a child, a young boy.

"The museums are closed. Most of the stores are closed," Fateh said. "There is not much here to see."

A few blocks later, we hit a traffic jam. About half a dozen cars had stopped ahead of us in the lane of traffic. Fateh slowed, then stopped the car. It was a roadblock. When we reached the barricade, two young men, armed and dressed in uniforms, walked to the car window. Following Fateh's instructions, I looked down at my feet. Out of the corner of my eye, I saw Nazil lift up the papers and jacket that were lying around the car to allow the police to see the contents and the surface areas inside. The gendarmes smiled weakly, then waved us through.

"They seemed friendly," I said, as we picked up speed.

Nazil leaned forward over the seat back. "The gendarmes are decent, gentle people," he said. "They have been hurt by this too.

"I have a friend who is a gendarme," he continued. "The terrorists set him up. They knew that on this night my friend would be walking alone, without his gun. They knew where he would be walking and at what time. They hid in the bushes. When my friend walked by, the terrorists jumped out. One held a gun to my friend's head. 'Now you are going to die,' the terrorist said to my friend. He pulled the trigger. But the gun stuck. My friend's life was saved.

"The terrorists have connections," Nazil said. "They know people's routines and their plans. I do not know how they know so much, but they do. They know who is here, and when people are coming and leaving. If they do not already know you are here, they will soon learn of your visit."

We drove through town, winding our way down to the street that ran alongside the harbor. Soon, we reached another roadblock. Fateh stopped the car. I stared at my feet. Again Nazil showed the gendarmes the contents of the back seat. Again, the police waved us through.

"We have lost much," Nazil said. "Most of us have lost someone we love. We all know someone who has lost a loved one. We live in fear each day of losing our friends and families. And as you can see, we have also lost our freedom."

Fateh stopped at a gas station at the edge of town, then we headed to the country. Before long the street we were driving on turned into a coastal highway.

"I remember the day it started," Nazil said.

Fateh nodded.

"June 5, 1991," they said, almost in unison.

Nazil gave me a brief course in Algerian history. Algeria had been colonized by France. Following an eight-year revolutionary war, Algeria had finally won its independence in 1962. By the early nineties, the Islamic party had won preliminary elections and threatened to take control of the government. That's when the civil war began. Algeria had stopped fighting France, but its two main political parties, the secular National Liberation Front and the religious Islamic Salvation Front, had begun to fight each other.

On June 5, 1991, the president of Algeria declared martial law.

"That's when the first terrorist incidents occurred," Nazil said. "It started with one or two isolated bombings. Then terrorism became a way of life. A few years ago, the military took over the government."

"There was an earthquake here that killed five thousand people," Nazil said. "You have earthquakes, too, where you live. But our real national disaster here is terrorism. It has now taken somewhere between ten and sixty thousand lives."

"I noticed the price on the gas pumps," I said, after a while. "It's 1.45 *dinars* a liter. Gas costs more here than it does in the United States and it's your leading export. Why is gasoline so expensive here? Doesn't that make your people angry?"

"Yes," Nazil said. "My people are angry. They're angry at the government. They're angry at the rich. They're not sure who let them down, but they know they've been betrayed."

We drove for a while, then Fateh pulled off the highway into a parking lot by a shopping complex. I opened the car door and started to get out. Fateh immediately reached across me and pulled my door shut. Then he just sat there.

"Mafateh is afraid," Nazil said. "Always afraid."

Fateh and Nazil spoke to each other for a while in Arabic. Then Nazil exhaled deeply, and explained to me what he and Fateh had been discussing. "Mafateh's fiancée was killed a year ago," Nazil said. "A bomb blew up the bus she was riding on. Now Mafateh always thinks it is going to happen again. He is afraid the terrorists will kill someone he loves or him next. I told him it was safe for us to get out and walk around for a while."

We got out of the car and walked around the shopping center. All the stores were closed and boarded up. Nazil led us around the side of the shopping complex. Then Fateh and I followed him down a dirt path that led to the sea. We scaled, single file, a stone pier that extended into the water. We walked as far as we could, then we all sat down on the rocks.

Sitting on the edge of the pier, Fateh now appeared almost relaxed for the first time this day.

"I'm sorry you lost your girlfriend," I said after a while.

"I was at her mother's house when it happened," he said quietly. "We were waiting for her to come home for dinner. The telephone rang. Her mother answered. When she dropped the phone and began to cry, I knew my girlfriend was dead."

"It hurts to lose someone in one moment," I said, "to have them ripped out of your life . . ."

He nodded.

We sat for a while, not talking. When three men approached the end of the pier, we simultaneously stood up and hurriedly returned to the car.

Fateh pulled the car onto the highway. A short time later, he exited again. This time he pulled into a parking area outside a park. Fateh reluctantly and nervously got out of the car. Nazil and I followed. The three of us walked across the lot to the park entrance.

A young couple, a man and a woman, sat in their car with the door open at the end of the lot. I felt a wave of fear rise in all three of us as we passed their vehicle. We entered the park, then walked at a brisk pace through the littered, almost vacant field. The land felt barren and untended. Even the trees felt strangely lifeless.

We walked to the park's recreation center. It was closed. We stood there looking at the closed facility for a moment. Then we turned around and headed back through the park to the car. After fixing the seat and rolling the car to start it, Fateh pulled back onto the highway. He continued to drive away from the city toward the looming hills.

Nazil pointed to the hills. "That's where the terrorist camps are," he said. "That's where they run to. That's where they train and live.

"It used to be that when a young man grew up, he made a decision to go to college, or go to work, or go into the military," Nazil explained. "Now there are two choices. Does he join the military? Or become a terrorist? The young men of our country take that decision very seriously.

"I have two friends. They were best friends. They played together as children in each other's homes. They knew each other's mothers. As they grew, one decided to join the military. The other decided to become a terrorist. They knew, as they were growing up, what they were going to be."

Nazil paused as he struggled to find just the right words to express his thoughts. "Each became . . . how do you say it . . . *dedicated* to his choice. When they reached eighteen, one of the men joined the military. The other ran for the hills to become a terrorist. Being a terrorist *was* his ambition.

"Just a few weeks ago, the man who had become a terrorist sneaked into the home of his friend, the one who had joined the military. His friend's mother was in the kitchen cooking. He crept up behind her. 'I'm going to kill him someday,' he whispered in her ear. 'You know that, don't you?' Then the terrorist ran out the door.

"They think their power comes from strength. They think power comes from guns, from killing people, from hurting people. That's not power," Nazil said, shaking his head.

"I don't know what makes them do it," he said. "They must be taking drugs. People would have to be using drugs to slit throats and kill people without thinking about it."

Fateh nodded.

After driving for about half an hour, Fateh again exited the highway. We were in a seaside resort town. Nazil explained that before the days of terrorism, people had crowded to this village for luxury vacations and fun weekend outings.

Now the streets were almost deserted. Most of the shops were closed. We walked down the sidewalk for a few blocks, past the locked or boarded-up storefronts. Occasionally, we encountered people—mostly men—who hurriedly walked by us. When we did, I continued to follow Fateh's instructions, avoiding all eye contact and looking down at my feet.

By now, my role as a subordinate woman—one who didn't speak or look directly into the eyes of anyone—felt oddly comfortable, almost familiar. It ran deeper than just following Mafateh's instructions or trying to avert an attack. I saw that it was frighteningly easy to dance to the rhythm of a culture and—almost by osmosis—adopt its beliefs and practices as our own.

I now understood the behavior of the woman at the reception desk at the hotel, the one who had told Mafateh about me—the one who had barely spoken to me and had avoided my eyes. She wasn't avoiding me. She was following the customs of her culture, dancing to her country's rhythm.

When we crossed the street at the end of the row of shops, we found ourselves at the gateway to a park. The gate was locked. We clung to the fence, trying to peek inside. In the courtyard just on the other side of the gate, untended plants in a sprawling garden had intertwined themselves around majestic Grecian ruins, crumbling stone reminders of Greece's influence in Algeria's rich history. We stared through the fence for a while, then turned and began walking back to the car.

"This is a fun day," Fateh said earnestly. "We're having a good day, aren't we? We went to the country."

Nazil and I nodded.

"Yes, Fateh," I said. "This is fun."

We got back in the car. Fateh again fixed the collapsed seat, rolled the car until it started, then headed back to the highway.

"We will drive down another road for a while," Fateh said.

He turned inland at a juncture, driving away from the sea, toward the ominous hills. After a while, he looped back in the direction of the city of Algiers. We drove past miles of expansive but desolate countryside, encountering few other vehicles along the way. Then, at a juncture where the intersecting road led directly to the hills, we pulled to a stop at a barricade.

This time I noticed I was holding my breath while I stared at the floor. I remembered the travel advisory warning about ambushes at false roadblocks. The gendarmes searched the car and waved us through.

"I love and respect my beautiful country," Nazil said after a while. "Terrible things have happened to my people. But the worst thing that has happened is that this has given them a spirit of vengeance.

"*Vengeance*," he said, "is not the purpose of what we are going through."

A heavy silence permeated the inside of the car. Then Nazil began speaking again.

"It is a tragedy what has happened to my country and my people. But the biggest damage is what's been done to our hearts. We don't even cry anymore when we hear of death. We have lived with the abnormal so long it's become normal. Our hearts have gone numb.

"That is the real tragedy of Algiers."

We drove for a while, looking at barren fields and rolling hills. Nazil explained that despite the country's fertile land, Algeria now imported most of its food.

He pointed to a large, windowless building tucked into the landscape on our left.

"That is where they take the terrorists who have been captured," he said. "Once, a doctor treated an injured terrorist. The police arrested the doctor and put *him* in jail. Two men I know were arguing about it the other day," Nazil said. "One of them could not understand why they would put a doctor in jail for treating an injured man."

I noticed stretch after stretch of buildings, tenements that looked abandoned or destroyed. I asked Nazil what had happened, if this was the result of terrorism or something else. He told me that most of the vacant buildings were projects that builders had begun, then abandoned when they ran out of money.

"This has gone on for so long," I said. "Do your people still have hope?"

"Hope?" Nazil said. "Yes, we have hope. But we do not hope for an improvement in our economy. We no longer hope for more agriculture, or more art. We only hope that one day the terrorism will stop."

Fateh turned onto the coastal highway. As we neared the city of Algiers, we all began to relax. Nazil started talking about college, about art classes he had taken, and about some of his friends from school. Soon after we reached the city limits, Fateh pulled the car to the side of the road by the harbor and told me we were dropping off Nazil. Fateh had to go to work.

Nazil told me how much he had enjoyed speaking English all day and that he hoped he had done a good job of expressing his thoughts to me.

I said that he had done an excellent job and thanked him.

I pulled my purse out from under the car seat. "Can I give you something, some money for your time today, as a gift, a way of saying thank you?" I asked Nazil.

He resolutely refused. "I could not take money," he said, shaking his head. "That would be wrong. It was a privilege to spend the day with you and tell you the story of Algeria and my people. Besides," he said, smiling, "we went for a drive in the country. We had fun."

I watched Nazil slip over the ruins, then disappear into a colony of homes by the sea. As Fateh drove us back to the hotel, I noticed for the first time how tensed my body was—and had been all day. Because of Ramadan, we had not eaten or drunk anything. I was getting thirsty. I wanted a drink of water.

"There's our zoo," Fateh said, as we neared the hotel. "It's closed now, but we have the oldest living alligator there," he said proudly.

We passed through the hotel's security barricade. Gendarmes searched the car one more time. Then Fateh parked and walked me to the hotel entrance. We stood there looking around at the guards, the barricades, and the treetops in the distance.

"Did you enjoy today?" Fateh asked.

"Yes, very much. Thank you," I said.

He smiled, and seemed pleased. I turned to him, put my hand over my heart, and *looked directly into his eyes.* "May God help your heart continue to heal from the loss of your love," I said.

Fateh looked at me. I saw and felt a strength in him I hadn't before seen. "I will pray that Allah is gentle with you, too," he said.

Fateh went to the hotel's employee entrance to report for work. I returned to my room. I was scheduled to be back in the lobby in one hour. Fateh had arranged several other events for me, including attending a holy Ramadan feast with a Berber family tomorrow evening to break the fast after sundown. My day tour of the Algerian countryside had ended.

Once in a while—not too often—a person crosses our path who, despite tremendous obstacles and pain, has managed to retain his or her identity, values, integrity, and faith in God—whether that person calls God "Allah," "Jehovah," or "God." That person knows what he or she believes and holds fast to those beliefs despite enormous pressure to do otherwise. And that person's decision to honor his or her values has little to do with what that person has received from life or from God. Although that person has not gotten what he or she has longed for, hoped for, desired, or deserved, he or she has not turned on God, or upon others. *He or she has not turned on himself or herself.*

There is a glowing power in that person that is irrefutable.

Being in that person's presence, even for a little while, changes us. We now have a paragon, a model, a jewel exemplar by which to gauge ourselves. We may not always live up to those standards, but we will forevermore be conscious of when we are falling short. And those few moments with that person will help us remember who and what we are striving to be.

That's what happened to me, in the heart of the vortex of terrorism on January 27, 1996, on my day tour of Algiers. I met a young man named Nazil. He told me the story of his country. He told me what he believed. And I saw a light that shone so brightly I would never again be the same.

In a land where people had lost their freedom and power, he had found a way to be free and he understood the meaning of power.

A true warrior had crossed my path.

D ID ANY OF THESE PEOPLE you met in Algiers give you anything to transport? Anything at all?" the Cairo interrogator demanded.

"Yes," I said. "They gave me some gifts."

"Show them to me now," she said.

I unlocked my suitcase, which was sitting on the large platform table between us. I showed her a pink, hand-embroidered Berber gown and a color poster of the *Casbah d'Alger*. Then I showed her my prized possession. It was a white cardboard year-at-a-time 1996 calendar. The names of the months and the days were inscribed in French. On the top of the calendar, above the months, was the national emblem for Algeria. It was also the emblem that had, by chance, become my personal seal for this trip—a crescent moon and star.

The woman interrogating me paused from her questioning for a moment and studied my itinerary.

"You were originally booked on a flight from Cairo to Greece. That was to be the last leg of your trip. Now it appears you have suddenly changed your plans and instead are flying from Cairo to Tel Aviv to Los Angeles. Why would you spend so much time in Algeria and Egypt, then at the last moment cancel the part of your travels that would have been such a *pleasant* vacation?"

"Oh, that," I said. "It surprised me, too. Let me explain."

chapter 5

Blackout

I unlocked the door to my hotel room and flopped down on the bed. My time in Algiers had filled up quickly. From the moment I met Fateh, I barely had time to sleep.

He had arranged two other tours for me besides my tour of the countryside. I had seen the highlight of Algerian night life—a barricaded indoor shopping center where cars lined up for miles waiting to be inspected by the gendarmes before entering.

I had seen the city by daylight, riding through the narrow, winding streets that led mysteriously into barren marketplaces and the *casbah*, streets conspicuously lacking the presence of women, streets fortified for battle by ramparts of armed guards.

I had just returned from the home of a local Berber family, neighbors and friends of Fateh. They had invited me to partake in a holy Ramadan feast at their house, to give thanks to Allah and break the day's fast after sundown. The family had not spoken English. Although I had no idea what I had eaten, the food was delicious. After the meal, they had handed me their family photo albums. I leafed through the pages, perusing a personal pictorial history echoing the same themes I had come across at the Museum of Man in Paris—birth, marriage, family, religion, and, just outside the windows of the French tenement where I sat, the threat of death. Then, before I left, the family had plied me with gifts. *"La Berber tradition,"* they had said, joyously placing present after present in my lap.

Back at the hotel, I looked at the bag of gifts lying on the floor next to the bed. The people of Algiers had opened their homes and their hearts to me. In this city where only a few days ago I thought I would be confined to my room, I had done and seen so much. This was to be my last evening here. I was scheduled to fly out in the morning—the only flight to Casablanca for several days. Now I wondered if I should cancel my flight, maybe leave later in the week.

I went into the bathroom and began to draw a bath. As I bent over the tub, adjusting the temperature of the hot water, the lights in the hotel room dimmed, flickered, then extinguished. I edged toward the door leading to the outside corridor, then opened it a crack. All the lights in the hotel were off.

It was a blackout.

A flickering of terror ran through my veins as Nazil's words flashed through my mind. *They know of things. They know who is coming and when they are leaving. If they do not already know you are here, they will soon learn.*

The darkened hallways outside my room were quiet, still. All I could hear was the sound of the water running into the tub, and the pounding of my heart. I closed the door, then leaned against it. Moments passed, slowly. The lights came back on. I finished drawing my bath, then packed my backpack. I *was* in the midst of a civil war. When Fateh had first knocked on my door, I had taken a deep breath and dived under the surface. Now I was running out of air.

It was time to go.

The next morning I slipped out of the city at dawn. As my plane took off, I stared out the window. I had never seen a country as beautiful as Algeria. Despite its beauty, the landscape emanated a haunting desolation. It was as if the earth itself—even the trees and foliage—had absorbed the pain and despondency of the people who inhabited it.

I felt relieved when the plane landed in Casablanca. My time in Algeria had been enlightening but stressful. I was ready to get back to life, vitality, and freedom—freedom especially from the imminent dangers of terrorism. I hailed a cab back to the hotel where I had stored my luggage.

"Je returnez! Je returnez!" I said to the desk clerk, a large frowning man wearing a caftan. He was yet another person who had scowled at the idea of my trip to Algeria. Now, he smiled slightly—at my safe return and, I guessed, at my illiterate use of the French language.

I checked into my room, feeling a strange mixture of emotions as I changed clothes and repacked my luggage. Algeria had tapped into some mysterious part of me. My time there now felt surrealistic. I wasn't certain I had been there. Nor was I completely certain I had survived. My experience there had ruffled ever so slightly the edges of the boundaries that keep reality so firmly and neatly in place.

I also felt energized. At the beginning of this trip, I had spent the better part of my few days in Paris hiding out in my room feeling intimidated by the luxury, beauty, and tinge of elitism that surrounded me. When I had finally ventured out of my room into the lobby, I had sat precariously on the edge of a velvet high-backed chair. A security guard had approached me and asked if I belonged there. I showed him my room key and said, "Yes, I do." Then I had gone out and done a few things. Now, the repression and confinement of Algeria made me even more determined to see and do as much as I could on the rest of this trip. I felt a new surge of power, a new appreciation for freedom. I belonged here, too. And I was going to act like it.

I immediately began planning an afternoon outing to Rabat, Morocco's capital. On my way to the taxi stand, I went into the restaurant in the hotel lobby and ordered a café au lait.

The same man who had served me the last time again brought me a silver tray containing a demitasse of espresso and a small pitcher of warm milk. I eyed that pitcher suspiciously. As I poured that warm milk into my coffee, I knew I shouldn't.

Until now, I had been arduously monitoring everything I ate and drank on this trip to try to prevent myself from getting sick. Except for the Ramadan feast in Algiers, I had barely tasted any of the succulent food.

But it wasn't just over here that I had been monitoring my intake. For the past six years or more, most of the people I knew, including myself, had devoted themselves to eating healthy. It was part of a larger process that was taking place—a detoxification, a cleansing, a fasting of sorts—as people developed a higher consciousness about what they ate and absorbed into their bodies. I could barely remember the days when food was just food, and if it tasted good, I ate it. Now, the rule of thumb was what the dumpy doctor in a "Wizard of Id" cartoon had told his patient: if it tastes good, spit it out. There were so many rules to follow, including my own. There were so many prohibitions against so many things. Lately, especially, it seemed as if everything I wanted I couldn't have.

So I drank every last sip of the espresso and warm milk.

On the sixty-mile drive to Rabat my stomach began to ache.

The taxi pulled into a lot outside a sprawling palace and courtyard. The driver then located a guide who offered to walk me through the typical tourist attractions. The guide was a stout old man with dark, sun-wrinkled skin and a missing front tooth. He told me to call him Tommy, but I knew that wasn't his name. It was just an easy word for Americans to pronounce. He told me if I liked what he showed me, I could pay him what I thought the tour was worth at the end of it.

We walked around the king's palace and the building where the king's children were tutored. Then we visited a sacred tomb site. The tomb was a two-story building burnished in gold and guarded by the police. Inside the building, a wraparound balcony overlooked an ornate coffin. Standing there, I had the strangest feeling that I was brushing against an opening between this world and the afterlife.

We left the tomb and walked and walked. My stomach hurt more with each step. Finally, we entered a large, terraced garden area. I realized how much I had missed nature on this trip. Except for my stressful visit to the Algerian countryside, I had spent most of my time in hotel rooms, crowded cities, and airports.

Tommy pointed to a large bird nesting on top of one of the crumbling columns of rock. "Look! I think it's a stork," he said.

We paused a moment to watch the bird.

By now, it was getting to be late afternoon. Tommy looked tired. I suspected he was hungry. Occasionally, I saw him sneaking peeks at his watch.

The dedication I had observed in the Muslims during my travels throughout the Arab world impressed me. The word "Islam," I would later learn, means "surrender or submission to the will of God." I was acutely aware of the heightened and accelerated spirituality in the air as the culture went deeper into the month of Ramadan. But I also sensed the strain of the fast wearing on the people as I observed them carrying on their daily work. Thirty days is a long time to abstain.

As I watched Tommy pant and puff, walking down the garden path, I could see the effects of the elongated fast wearing on him, too.

"Are you getting hungry?"

"Yes," he said.

"Going for a month without eating or drinking all day must get tough," I said.

He nodded. "But it's good for you," he said, grimacing.

I agreed. "It's good for the body, good for the mind . . ."

"And good for the spirit," he said, finishing my sentence.

I trudged behind Tommy across the wide main
streets of Rabat into the entrance to the *Casbah des
Oudaia,* a seventeenth-century fortress hidden within the city near the shores of the Atlantic Ocean. As
we walked the narrow streets of the *casbah,* I pointed
to a small open market nestled between two houses.
I couldn't stand the pain in my stomach any longer. I
needed a large bottle of water.

We finished the tour. I thanked and paid Tommy,
then made the drive back to Casablanca, holding my
stomach all the way. By now, it felt as if I had swallowed a porcupine, quills and all.

Many substances, places, and people can be toxic
to us. Even other people's self-hatred, their beliefs
about themselves or us, can be poisonous. What's
around us and what we absorb into our bodies affects
us. If we insist on being around a toxic person or in-
gesting a substance that's toxic to us, we can develop
an allergic-like reaction. Our bodies twist and con-
tort, become out of alignment and balance. We can
become confused, foggy, even sick. Our sense of
power diminishes. Toxic substances, toxic people,
and toxic beliefs can weaken people, just as the
mythical kryptonite weakened Superman.

Before I understood this, I had spent much of my
life turning on myself instead of backing away from

whatever was poisonous. If I just try harder, do better, be more, be different, I can handle this, I had thought. It had taken me a long time to learn that the lesson wasn't *handling* toxicity. It was learning to respect what was toxic to me.

There is a feeling that comes—a gentle hit of recognition—when something is right for us. Sometimes the response is almost electric. Other times it's more subtle. The body simply feels at peace. There is a different feeling that comes when something is wrong for us, when a person, place, thing, emotion, decision, or substance is toxic to us. That feeling can be either a strong negative reaction, a nagging sense that something is not quite right, or a blank response—we don't feel anything. It had taken me years to learn to detect my intuitive, bodily responses. Sometimes I still denied and ignored them, thinking I could just plow through on willpower, desire, and mental fortitude. And I still had my blind spots—those places in me that drove me straight to what I *knew* I was allergic to.

I had survived the terrorists in Algeria. But I did myself in when I ignored my instincts in Casablanca. I had broken my own rule: "Don't drink the milk."

When I returned to my room at the hotel in Casablanca, I dug through my suitcases and found some herbs for my stomach that I had brought for an emergency such as this.

I downed a handful, then walked to the window and opened the curtains. I saw all the same sights I had seen before, the first time I was here. Veiled women and dark-eyed men crowded the city streets. The noise from radios, cars, and ship horns blared up through the window. Soot covered all the buildings—the modern high-rises and the old Arabian shops. Maurice, my friend from America, had been right. Casablanca was indeed a dirty seaport city. But it had become more than that. Now, it had become a safe harbor and a home.

My time here was ending. Soon I would be leaving for Cairo, Egypt. The energy of this trip was about to shift again. I had no idea what was coming, no inkling of what was in store. For just a moment, clutching my stomach, I wondered if I should cancel my plans and return to America. That thought passed quickly. I was in way too deep. There was no turning back.

I had survived my initiation in the vortex of terrorism in Algeria. I had made my peace with Morocco. Now I was about to move into my indoctrination into the ancient Egyptian mystery school.

I STILL DO NOT UNDERSTAND why you would spend so much time in the countries you did and then suddenly decide not to fly to Greece for the luxury part of your vacation," my interrogator in Cairo said.

"It was probably a combination of my allergy to dairy products and the difference in the way milk is treated here," I said. "But I got sick from drinking the milk."

I hated myself for what happened next. I started to cry. "I haven't done anything wrong," I said. "I'm tired. I'm sick. And I just want to go home."

The woman looked at me. She began talking to the man standing next to her, again in a language I couldn't understand. Then she turned to me. "I'm sorry this had to take so long," she said. "You can go now."

As suddenly as this interrogation began, it ended. I didn't understand what had just happened, but it was over. The flight to Tel Aviv had been de-layed for several hours. The interrogation had lasted most of that time. I sat in the gate area waiting for the boarding call and wondered if I was being watched or observed.

I relaxed when I reached the Tel Aviv airport. It felt airy, much lighter than the airports of North Africa, more like being inside a Lutheran church than a terminal. Because I was changing airlines here, I had to claim my luggage, pass through customs, and recheck my luggage on the flight to America. Even with the delay in Cairo, I still had over four hours before my plane departed. I gathered my suitcases, found a cart, and began pushing my way through the sprawling airport. When I passed the all-night restaurant, I decided to stop for a bagel.

I looked around, noticing the enchanting demeanor and rituals of the people around me. I wished I had scheduled some time here on my trip. Even from this limited exposure to Israel—sitting in the airport restaurant in the middle of the night—I found the culture enticing.

This was the land where the Christ lived, walked, and did His work.

I remembered a conversation with Nichole shortly before I left on this trip. It happened one day when I asked her to look up a particular Bible verse for me. She copied the verse onto a piece of paper, brought it to me, and began reading aloud.

*"Matthew 22:35," she said. "Then one of them, which was a lawyer, asked him a question, tempting him, and saying, 'Master, which is the great command- ment in the law?' Jesus said unto him, 'Thou shalt love the Lord thy God with all thy heart, and with all thy soul, and with all thy mind. This is the first and great commandment. And the second is **like . . . unto . . . it.'** "*

Nichole stopped struggling with the thick text and just looked at me. "I didn't know they talked like Valley Girls back then," she said.

"Keep reading," I said.

" 'Thou shalt love thy neighbour as thyself.' "

"Most people don't know how much they hate themselves," she said a short time later.

I agreed.

"When you tell people you don't like yourself, they just scrunch their face and say things like 'How can you not love yourself?' Or they say, 'I don't understand that because I really love myself.' But then you look at them and you know that's not true. They hate them- selves, too. They just don't know it.

"It used to bother me why some people had to go through so much pain in life and be so aware of it, and other people were just happy to go bowling," she said, almost as an afterthought. "For a long time, I thought

maybe we were being punished for something. But now, it doesn't bother me anymore."

"Why?" I asked.

"I don't think people who have a lot of pain are being punished," she said. "I believe they're the chosen ones."

I finished my bagel and reached the security checkpoint seconds before a tour group of about one hundred Japanese travelers arrived. One of the security guards, a woman, pointed to a lane on the right and told me to stand there. She lined the tour group up in the lane next to me. Then she began checking them through first. I looked at the line next to me. This was going to be a long night.

I motioned to the security guard.

"Actually, I was here before them," I said. "It's late. I'm tired. And you told me to stand here. But no one is checking me through. Am I in the wrong lane?" I asked.

"No, you're not," she said. "Please come with me."

She led me to a table removed from the crowd, at the far end of the room. On the other side of the counter stood two uniformed women. They both looked like college girls. One of them, the one with shoulder-length chestnut-brown hair, did all the talking.

She started by asking simple questions: how long had I been traveling, who was I traveling with, what was I doing, an American woman, traveling alone. To each of my answers, she responded with an unemotional "I see."

She asked to see proof that I was a writer. I said I didn't have any. She wanted to know why I didn't bring any of my books with me. I told her I had considered it, but I had already overpacked and had no room. She asked why I had come to Tel Aviv and who I was seeing or meeting here. I told her no one, I was changing planes, not leaving the airport; it was a stopover on my way back to the United States.

Then she returned to the subject of proving I was a writer. I showed her a few pieces of paper, letters to and from my publisher, and some faxes concerning my work.

"What have you written?" she asked.

"Hundreds of newspaper articles," I said. Shit, I thought. Wrong answer. "And eight books. The one I'm best known for in my country is *Codependent No More*."

"What's that?" she asked.

"A miracle," I said.

She just looked at me.

"It's about learning to take care of yourself when the people around you would rather you didn't because they want you to take care of them. And so would you—rather take care of them instead of yourself," I said.

"What's the name of the book you're working on now?" she asked.

"Stop Being Mean to Yourself."

"What does *that* mean?" she asked.

By now, I felt singled out, persecuted, angry. And mean. How could anyone, even her, not know what that meant? Convinced she was deliberately tormenting me, I took a deep breath, leaned closer, only inches from her face, and began talking *at* her.

"We live in a world that's very mean-spirited," I said. "There's a lot of it going around. People are scared. They don't know what to expect. But the problem is, in a world that's already mean-spirited enough, many of us have taken all that anger and all that fear and turned it on ourselves. We're being mean to ourselves. This is a book about not doing that."

She paused. I thought we were done. Then she came right back at me. "What could the people in the countries you've visited possibly have to do with that?" she asked.

"We have things—experiences, emotions, lessons—in common with all people," I said quietly, "no
matter where we live."

"Explain that, please," she said.

I took a deep breath. Here we go again, I thought.

chapter 6

Shisha

Cairo, the densely populated capital of Egypt and the largest city in Africa, extends from the east bank of the Nile to the edge of the Sahara—the vastest desert on this planet, a desert almost the size of the United States of America. In this city of extreme contrast between old Arab architecture and glistening, new high-rise buildings, many people depend as much on horses, camels, and donkeys for transportation as they do on buses, cars, and airplanes. Islamic religion is the law of the land in this ancient center for trade, art, and the Muslim culture. While contemporary Cairo has become a Middle Eastern hub for publishing, radio, and television, some say the major export of this mystical desert capital is still life after death.

The moment I stepped off the plane in Cairo, I knew the lighter part of my travels had just begun. The heaviness—the terror and the basic survival issues of Algeria, the poverty and desperation of Morocco—lifted. After darting through the battlefields of Algiers, walking through the Cairo airport felt almost the same as being home in America.

I had arranged for a shuttle and a driver, who I was told would be a woman, to meet me at the airport; all I had to do was collect my luggage, pass through customs, and locate the car. As I waited in line to show my passport, I couldn't help noticing the signs plastered all over the walls. The huge posters with bold print were not to be ignored:

"WELCOME TO EGYPT. DRUG USERS WILL EITHER BE EXECUTED OR IMPRISONED FOR LIFE. HAVE A GOOD STAY."

Okay, I thought, I will *have a good stay*.

I showed the customs officer my passport, cleared the security check, then headed toward the front door of the airport. It feels so freeing not to have to be protected on my way to the hotel, I thought, remembering my experience at the Algerian airport.

Seconds after this thought crossed my mind, an extremely polite young man in a uniform darted across the room, intercepting me. He asked where I was going. I said I had been told a shuttle and a woman driver were waiting out front for me. He looked at me as if I had lost my mind.

"I don't think so," he said.

I insisted that I had a driver waiting. He said he would watch my luggage while I checked. I walked to the street in front of the airport and looked around. I did not see a shuttle. I did not see anybody looking for me—particularly a woman. I walked back into the airport to the young man and my luggage.

"The shuttle isn't here yet," I said. "I'll wait."

"I'll find you a driver," he insisted.

I walked over to the money booth to exchange some American currency for Egyptian pounds. The polite young man went to arrange a taxi. When I returned to my luggage, five polite young men now waited to escort me and my baggage to the taxi. Each young man at least touched one piece of my luggage. Then each polite young man stuck his hand out, waiting for a gratuity. This could get expensive, I thought, sticking a few pounds in each outstretched palm.

I entered the cab, gave the driver the name of the downtown hotel where I had reservations, then settled back in the seat. The driver pulled out into traffic. Soon I was on the edge of my seat.

There were no marked lanes for traffic, at least none that drivers observed. Cars darted into oncoming traffic, passing on either the left or the right side. Drivers insisted on squeezing through between lanes of cars, making their own lane in a space where there wasn't enough room for a motorcycle. Cars turned left or right whenever they felt like it, from whatever lane they were in, despite the implications of any oncoming traffic.

I leaned toward the driver.

"This is like playing bumper cars," I said.

He smiled and nodded.

In spite of the apparent chaos, there seemed to be a rhythm, a flow, to the driving. I didn't see that many accidents, and I was checking. I guessed it would be okay. I leaned back and let myself go for the ride.

Although it was late, almost 10:00 P.M., when we reached the hotel, I wasn't tired. Something or someone was calling to me. *Later I would learn it was both.*

I asked the driver to wait for me, then quickly checked into my room and returned to the taxi.

The driver, an intense, dark-skinned, chain-smoking man of medium build whom I guessed to be about fifty, spoke a thick combination of Arabic and broken English. I didn't know exactly where to tell him to go, or where there was to go here in Cairo. Except for my hotel reservations, I was traveling on instinct. He started driving around aimlessly. As the night had worn on, the traffic had increased. The streets now felt frenzied. Soon so did I.

After about ten minutes, we drove into a quieter part of town. Wherever we were, it felt calmer, more peaceful. Suddenly, I saw a section of the Nile—the river that flows north, the longest river in the world, Cleopatra's river. "Ahh," I said. Just as suddenly, the driver swerved away from the river and headed in the direction we had just come from, back into the chaos. He drove around and around. It looked to me as if we were going in circles. I began pointing in a direction; I wasn't certain why.

"Go that way," I said. "Drive there!"

He followed my orders. Soon we began clearing the intense traffic of the downtown area. I felt a different energy pulling me toward it.

"Keep going," I said.

Suddenly, in the distance, I saw them—rising above the skyline, lit with colored lights for the night shows, the tips of the ancient pyramids of Giza. Now I knew what was beckoning me.

"That's it," I said. "That's why I'm here."

He drove past the tourist stands to a fenced area on the other side of the pyramids. I jumped out of the car and ran to the chain-link fence. The three great pyramids of the pharaohs—Khufu, Khafre, and Menkure—rose majestically from the dust of the Sahara. The warm night winds blew gentle billows of sand through the air. My black shoes turned light brown from the dust as I soaked up the energy from these mysterious monuments to the afterworld. In half an hour, I had moved from the pandemonium and tumult of the swarming city of Cairo to the edge of the Sahara Desert and one of the Seven Ancient Wonders of this world.

I stood, my nose to the fence, and gaped.

I had just entered one of the most powerful spiritual vortexes on this planet.

Only a few moments later, I felt a sinister presence impinging on my reverie. I turned around. Three swarthy men in their late twenties or thirties were moving menacingly toward me—coming at me, cornering me against the fence.

I frantically searched for my driver. He was standing back about twenty feet away from me, watching. I looked at him, flashing an unspoken message to help. He avoided my eyes, turned his back on me, and began to walk away.

My God. I couldn't believe it. He was leaving me for dead.

I couldn't speak. I couldn't find words. It felt as if my throat was closing. I felt paralyzed. I stood frozen, watching it happen. The men were only feet from me.

"Don't abandon me!"

I don't know if I screamed the words or transferred them telepathically.

The driver heard.

He stopped in his tracks and spun around. Then he looked at me with the oddest expression, as if he was relenting or changing his mind. I felt a flickering of recognition—something almost as ancient as the pyramids—about this subtle transaction. In a heartbeat, just as the men were about to strike, the driver was back at my side. He put his arm around my waist, pushed the men aside, and whisked me back to the cab.

Some threshold had been crossed, some form of communication established, between this furtive, dark-eyed, chain-smoking man and myself. He circled back around the pyramids, into the heart of a settlement I would later come to know as Giza. He drove past blocks of small Arab shops, now closed for the night, then turned onto Sphinx Street. After a few moments, he pulled into a sprawling sandlot and parked the car at the end of it, in front of a small shop.

The plain sign in the shop's lit window announced its name: Lotus Palace Perfumes. Tiny, ornate bottles of every shape and color—pink, red, gold, green, and purple—lined the windows and shelves. The door was open. Several men sat on a bench in front of the store. On the other side of the lot, in front of a tenement, a camel knelt on the ground, smiling and chewing hay while a woman vigorously groomed him.

One of the men sitting on the bench rose, walked to the cab, and opened my door.

"Welcome to the village of Giza," he said. "My name is Essam."

I looked at the man holding open the door. He wore a long, dark skirt over his pants. He was of medium height, slightly rotund, with hair that had begun to thin. He had kind eyes, a sweet round face, and a gentle spirit. I stepped out of the taxi and offered him my hand.

We talked for a minute. I told him where I was from, and that I had just arrived in Cairo an hour ago.

"Would you like to see the pyramids?" Essam asked.

I said I would.

"Would you like to ride a camel over there?" he asked.

I swallowed hard, then said yes. "But it's so late," I said. "How much will it cost?"

"Don't worry," Essam said. "This is Ramadan, a time of giving, a time to remember Allah. You go to the pyramids, touch their powers, your first night here. When you return, you pay me what you think it was worth."

He smiled. "Have fun!"

I swung my right leg over the humped back of the biggest creature I had come across in my life. I held onto the saddle. The camel jerked upright from its knees, gently throwing me backwards. Then I started grinning and couldn't stop, as the camel clopped along the narrow passage next to the sandlot, down past a block of shops, then up the side of a mountain, and down onto the desert. A boy of about seventeen, Essam's nephew, rode next to me on a horse.

We rode to within a few hundred feet of the pyramids, then stopped. The Sahara surrounded me. In the distance, the glistening lights of Cairo touched the edge of the night sky. I sat on the camel, gazing out at the pyramids, the Sphinx, and the desert. The frenzy and fear I had felt earlier disappeared. I was safe.

After about twenty minutes, we clopped back to the perfume shop. Essam was waiting for me with a cup of hot Egyptian tea. He assured me it had been brewed with bottled water. He said he didn't want me to get sick.

I tipped the boy on the horse, the one who had accompanied me. I put a handful of pounds in Essam's hand and thanked him. He said I had given him too much money, and he returned half of it. We talked for a while. I told him I didn't know how long I would be in Cairo, maybe a few weeks. He said he would help in any way he could. I made plans to re-turn in a day or two, then asked the cab driver to take me back to the hotel.

From the moment I met him, I knew Essam would be a teacher and a friend.

Back in the cab, it took about fifteen minutes to reenter the chaotic downtown Cairo district. Before long, I spotted my hotel rising in the distance. We got closer and closer, then I saw the hotel disappear be-hind us.

"Where are we going?" I asked.

"You will come for coffee with me now," the driver said firmly.

"No thank you," I said. "I'm tired. Take me back to the hotel."

"You will come with me," he said.

He drove under a bridge, then parked the car in a small lot, way too small for the ten cars that were crammed in there. He walked to my door, opened it, took my hand, and guided me out.

"Where are we going?" I asked again.

"Coffee," he said brusquely.

"I don't want coffee," I said. "It's too late . . ."

He ignored me and kept walking, pulling me along by my hand.

We walked up a flight of stairs, over a walking bridge, down the stairs, and across a street. I was dusty from the desert, confused, scared, and curious. By now, my thigh-high stockings were bunched around my ankles, but we were walking too fast for me to pull them up. We rounded a corner and entered a section of the city that had no car traffic. Instead, people—hundreds, thousands of them—crowded the streets. They jammed so close together that there was no space between bodies. People touched those in front of and behind them as they moved along the street. Yet I saw and felt the same erratic rhythm here with this mass of people that I had observed with the cars. The driver and I were swept up by the throngs of people and moved along by the pulsating tempo of this gigantic conga line.

The sidewalks were crammed with old shops, piled one atop another. I saw silversmiths. Fruit stands flooded with dates and oranges. Clothing. Rugs. Every kind of Egyptian ware, product, and foodstuff imaginable. It had to be after midnight, yet all the shops were open. For the first time in all my travels through the Arab world, I saw women talking, walking, shopping. I was torn between gazing at the stores and their colorful displays, and vigorously trying to keep my place in line. Someone pinched my butt. I couldn't stop moving. I would have been trampled. I looked over my shoulder. A shrunken, gray-haired man about four feet tall and eighty years old grinned at me. He had no teeth. I glared, then turned around.

Suddenly I got it. Oh, I thought. This is the *souk*.

I remembered what the travel agent had said about the *souks*, the mysterious marketplaces of the Arab world. "They run for miles. People live in there. They're born, live, and die in there. Be careful. People can go in, and never come out."

"Is this the *souk?*" I screamed at my driver, talking slowly enough so he could understand me and loudly enough to be heard above the noise of the crowd.

He nodded. "The *souk,*" he said.

We walked block after block, going deeper and deeper into the *souk,* pulled along by the massive moving crowd. Finally, my driver steered me out of the main stream of traffic and led me up a flight of stairs into a small store. He guided me through the store onto a second-floor balcony. He pulled out a chair in front of a small table and said, "Sit."

I wanted to pull up my stockings, but I didn't know how I could possibly do that. They were completely around my ankles.

So I sat down. The driver sat down next to me. Minutes later, a waiter came to the table. He seemed to know my driver. They talked in Arabic for a few minutes. Moments later, the waiter returned lugging the largest, most ornate, floor-standing water pipe, or hookah, I had ever seen in my life.

The driver lit the coals like an expert, took a big, deep puff, then passed the hookah tube to me.

I looked around the balcony. There were four or five other small tables, occupied mostly by men. All of them were smoking water pipes. Oh, my God, I thought. I am being drugged and kidnapped. It's all coming down, right now. I am watching it happen. I have just been spirited to the Egyptian equivalent of an opium den.

I wanted to be invisible on this trip but I didn't want to disappear.

For the second time that evening, I became paralyzed with fear. Again, I felt an ancient stirring within, this time a recollection of being powerless, unable to speak, helpless to defend myself.

Just a minute, I thought. I'm a forty-seven-year-old woman. What would they possibly want or do with me, even if they did get me?

I relaxed for just a moment, then flashed to the sign at the airport: DRUG USERS WILL EITHER BE EXECUTED OR IMPRISONED FOR LIFE. No matter what's coming down, this is not looking good, I thought. I have to get out of here. This is not a good thing.

I looked at my driver. He was looking at me, holding out the drawing tube to the hookah, offering it to me, waiting. My voice was paralyzed. My hands were sweating. I could neither speak nor move.

One night back home, I dreamt I was alone in a house that was about to be attacked by thieves. One of the doors was unsecured and could easily be accessed by anyone desiring entry. Three robbers stood outside planning and discussing the evil they intended to do. I saw the thieves. I heard them. But I couldn't speak and I couldn't get away. I felt helpless. I panicked. In my dream, I picked up the phone and dialed 911, the emergency number. No response. The phone rang into a void. I set the receiver in the cradle and just watched as the robbers discussed how they were going to enter through the unsecured door. They were laughing about the harm they intended to inflict once they entered. In my dream—just as at the pyramids and now in the souk—I watched, fully aware it was happening yet unable to speak up or protect myself. "Help," I screamed in my dream. At first my cry sounded weak; then my voice became louder. Finally, I screamed "Help!" so loudly I woke myself up and startled my bird. Minutes later, while I sat in my living room trying to make sense of the dream, I could still feel the resounding vibrations from my shriek.

Still back home, days later, I had a similar dream. In that dream, a woman entered my home uninvited. I knew she was not of good will; she meant harm. I didn't want her there, but she just walked into my house anyway, as though she had a right to be there. Again, I just watched, speechless and paralyzed. Finally, I mustered up the courage, the energy, and the power to push through the block and speak the words stuck in my throat. "Get out," I finally screamed, again waking myself up. "Get out!"

At home, my dreams then took me back to my childhood, and to one of several incidents that I wished were only dreams. When I was twelve years old, I often baby-sat for the children of people who lived in my neighborhood. One family I frequently worked for was a well-respected, friendly couple with three young children. I liked their house. It wasn't fancy, but it was clean and pretty. I liked their children. And they paid me fifty cents an hour—good money at the time. One New Year's Eve when I was baby-sitting, they returned home late. I was asleep on the couch when they arrived. The woman disappeared into the bedroom. I was too tired, it was too late, I was too young to notice how drunk the man was—too drunk to drive me home. On the way home, instead of turning at the corner where I lived, he continued to drive. After a few blocks, he parked the car. In the next instant, he was on top of me, all over me, pulling off my clothes. "Stop," I wanted to scream. "Get off! Get away!" I couldn't. Those words had stuck in my throat, too. I lay there frozen, until he finished, zipped up his pants, and drove me home.

Now, in the second-floor balcony in the small Arab shop in the heart of the *souk* in Cairo, Egypt, I forced myself to push words through that same block in my throat. The words gurgled out weakly at first, like water just coming out of a rusty spigot. But they came out.

"Hashish?" I asked, pointing at the water pipe. "Is that hashish?"

The driver looked at me, leaned back in his chair, and started laughing. "Hashish? No!" he said. "Not hashish. *Shisha.*"

"*Shisha?*" I said.

"*Shisha,*" he said.

"What's *shisha?*" I asked.

"Egyptian tobacco. Soaked in honey. Smoke it in *shisha,*" he said, pointing to the pipe. "It's good."

"Tobacco?" I said, pointing to the pipe. "That's what that is?"

"*Shisha,*" he said. "Try some."

I looked at the other people on the balcony. This time I studied them more closely. They were all drinking fruit drinks and teas. I scanned the menu on the wall, trying to read the words. I was in a juice bar, the Egyptian equivalent of a health food store. The only difference was that here, health food stores

apparently served juice with a water pipe and tobacco. I sniffed the *shisha*. It smelled good, like pure
pipe tobacco. I thought about trying a puff, then, remembering my experience with the milk in Morocco,
decided against it. My stomach still hurt. I ordered a
glass of mango juice and sat back.

*Ten years ago, a psychic—a gypsy I knew back
then—wanted to give me a reading. Her jewelry clank-
ing, she dug out her crystal ball. Her eyes glazed over
as she began gazing into the glass sphere. After a few
moments, she looked into my eyes and made her
solemn extrasensory pronouncement.*

*"I see—I'm getting—that you don't really love
yourself," she said.*

"Tell me something I don't know," I said to her.

Although I probably wouldn't make it into the
Howard Stern Self-Loathing Hall of Fame, I knew I
had moments when I came close. I had my bouts
with self-contempt, fear, and at times downright self-
hatred. I was as prone to betray and deceive myself as
I was to allow others to betray or misuse me. But I
didn't see that great a difference between myself and
most of the people I knew.

The gypsy's words stuck with me for years, implanted in my psyche like a foreign object. I agreed
with her; I probably didn't love myself as much as I

should. The problem was, I loved myself as much as I could and as much as I knew how.

Looking back, it was probably then that I began to glorify the idea of self-love, turning it into an ideal. I searched for it as if it was the Holy Grail—hidden, just out of reach, yet a worthy and noble cause. I began to believe that self-love was a static condition, like reaching majority. Once a person is over twenty-one, that person is over twenty-one forever. I envisioned running around like a Stepford wife, loving myself all the time, not feeling any emotions, not feeling tormented, just glowingly, contentedly (and I might add *nauseatingly*) loving myself. That description didn't apply to me and probably never would. Yes, I decided over the years, the gypsy was right. I don't love myself.

It's better for me not to consult fortune-tellers anymore, not because they're bad, wrong, or necessarily evil, but because I'm too susceptible. It's easy enough for me to hand my golden ball of power over to people I can see. I'm a walking target for unseen entities or those that claim privileged connection to unseen powers. And I have enough misconceptions of my own to unravel—especially about love.

In Aikido, the martial art I've been studying, the student learns to be strong yet gentle, relaxed yet deeply alert and intuitive. The word "Aikido" means "the way of harmonizing and unifying oneself with the spirit and energy of the universe." Learning Aikido is a lifetime commitment. And a student can practice and keep getting better at it as long as she or he lives. The light in that golden ball of power, the one each of us has in our solar plexus, doesn't deteriorate with age. It increases as the student acquires and practices certain disciplines, like rolling forward, rolling backward, and learning to breathe. One day my teacher told me that O Sensei, Aikido's founder, did demonstrations until the day he died. The master even got out of his hospital bed and did a final demonstration of his skills shortly before his death.

These same ideas have now replaced my idealized notions about self-love. Loving ourselves requires a lifetime commitment. It is the art of growing in our ability to live in harmony with ourselves and the spirit and energy of the universe. And if we keep practicing certain disciplines—including breathing—we can get better at it as long as we live. Our golden ball of power just keeps glowing more brightly.

Somewhere between abject self-loathing and the grandiosity and narcissism of believing that we're impervious and know best what everyone else in the world should do is that sacred space we call self-love. It is a portal and a gateway. How we find it is a mystery; so is its power to get us to the next place.

While some people say that fear, hatred, and contempt are the opposites of love, I don't see life as such a tidy package of dualities anymore. I believe our fear, hatred, and contempt—even those moments of contempt for ourselves that choke us up and paralyze our voice—are only barriers, obstacles, and blocks to work through on the way to finding that sacred space.

The whirling vortex of energy in Cairo had taken me, in my first few hours here, to the Nile, to the ancient mystical pyramids, to the Sphinx, to Essam, and to the *souk*. But it had also taken me back to myself. As I sat on the second-floor balcony in the Arabian health food store sipping my mango drink, the message became clear. *When life turns on you, whether that turning is real or imagined, clear your throat. Speak up. Tell someone who cares. Most of all, learn to tell yourself.* The wisdom of the ages may be buried in the tombs of Giza, but it's also buried deep within each of us.

I looked down at the bustling street below. That's when I saw him, across the street from us. I had noticed him for the first time when I moved through the crowded streets on my way here. He caught my interest then. Now I found him compelling. I pointed to the man, then pulled at my driver's arm, trying to get him to put down the *shisha*.

"Who's that?" I asked. "And what's he doing?"

I LOOKED AROUND THE ROOM where I stood in the Tel Aviv airport. By now, the crowds of travelers had thinned to one or two people. The entire line of Japanese tourists had cleared security. The subtle methods of the interrogators had sucked me in again.

My palms were sweating. I felt frightened, persecuted, and trapped. I hadn't felt this under the gun for a long time. What was I supposed to do? I couldn't say "I don't want to discuss this" and walk away. It wasn't like talking to the media, or a feisty lover.

I had no choice but to continue telling my story.

chapter 7

The Sandlot

I returned to Essam at the Lotus Palace Perfumes the following day.

Lotus Palace Perfumes had belonged to Essam's father until the father died. Now Essam and his brother ran the store. They were gentle men and devout Muslims. Although the Ramadan fast continued throughout my stay in Egypt, Essam made sure I ate each day. He would have the women of his house prepare a typical Egyptian lunch, and the children would bring it to the store: a loaf of bread, slabs of cheese, dates, hot tea brewed with bottled water, and fruit—an orange or a tangerine—to finish the meal and cleanse the palate.

Sometimes at the end of the day, Essam would invite me to join him and any men friends from the village who wandered by for the sundown feast to break the day's fast. By then the men would be ravenous. The boys would scurry from the sprawling house next to the shop carrying platters of chicken, rice, and many other Egyptian dishes. Soon the small perfume store would turn into a dining room. We would feast, as Essam passed the platters from person to person, making certain we tasted each succulent dish.

Most of the activity, however, took place outside in the sandlot on the wooden bench in front of the store. During the day and long into the evening hours, the men would gather at the bench. The boys would play and ride horses and donkeys in the lot. Occasionally, I would see a woman vigorously grooming a camel, but to see a woman here was rare. Sometimes Essam would push the stand bearing the small black and white television set outside and position it alongside the bench. Then all the men and male children would gather around and watch.

Although I stayed at a hotel in Cairo, then later moved to a hotel in Giza, the dusty sandlot with the boys and the men, the camels and the horses, the bread and the cheese, and sometimes the black and white television became my home in Egypt.

On this day, immediately upon my arrival when my taxi squealed to a stop in the dust in front of the store, Essam scurried to the side of the cab. When I started to pay the driver the fare he asked, Essam scowled, shook his head no, and pulled me aside.

"He is overcharging you," Essam said. "Do not just give people the amount of money they ask for. It is considered a point of honor here to negotiate the price of everything. You will not be respected unless you do. Give him half of what he asks. No more," Essam said firmly.

I did what Essam said. Essam and I were satisfied. Eventually the driver was, too.

The taxi driver from the night before had told me about the man in the *souk*, the one I had found so compelling.

I first saw the man as I was darting through the crowded streets. Actually, I saw his stick first, as the long, thin rod came whipping through the air, rapping certain people about the head and shoulders.

I cringed and ducked when I saw the man whack a shifty-looking young man just a few feet away from me. That's getting close, I thought. I wondered if I was next. Something told me not to worry.

Later, looking down over the crowds from the balcony at the juice bar, I could see the man with the stick more clearly. He sat on a stool across the street from me on the corner of a busy intersection, perched just high enough so that he was slightly elevated above the heads of the crowd. I watched, mesmerized. At first it looked as if he was randomly striking out at people with the long, thin, wooden rod he held in his hand. Soon, I began to notice a rhythm to his whacks, the same chaotic yet measured cadence I had seen in the traffic of Cairo's streets.

"He hits the bad guys," my driver explained matter-of-factly, when I tugged at his arm and asked him to tell me about this mysterious man. "There's bad guys out there," the driver said. "They steal. They rob. When the man hits them with the stick, the people know who the bad guys are. And it tells the bad guys to stop."

When I asked if the man with the stick worked for the police, the driver said that he didn't. From what I could discern from my driver's broken English, it was a *self-appointed mission. When I asked how the man with the stick knew who the bad guys were and who he should hit, the driver said, "He knows."*

I need one of those, I thought instantly. I need a stick.

So much of this civil war with myself had been over this issue. I wanted to attribute kind, generous, benevolent motives to many people and sometimes to the wrong people. That belief system didn't create a world that was nice and kind—it opened a door that let the bad guys in.

In the days to come, I would notice that many of the men and boys of the village of Giza carried a stick. Often, it was associated with riding and used to direct a horse, camel, or ass. But I began to see that the stick was more than a necessary tool. It was a symbol of protection and power.

Years ago, when I had started learning about setting limits, saying no—*getting a stick*—I thought it was something I would need to do for a short while. I assumed that as I progressed in my life, the situations where I would need to use my stick would decrease and eventually be eliminated. But at each new level of play, an abundance of new situations arose requiring that I pick up and use my stick. Some of these circumstances were obvious situations of manipulation, deceit, or chemical abuse. These situations were simple to deal with and easy to recognize. But many situations at the new levels were far more subtle. The energy patterns were similar. I'd feel off balance and confused. Something wouldn't feel right, then I would doubt whether I could trust myself and I would be uncertain about what to do next. But dealing with these situations became more complicated. Recognizing them was often tricky.

At first, this had caught me off guard. Slowly I began to understand that I needed to pay closer attention. From shopkeepers to healers to lovers, in personal life and in the business world, there are a wealth of people ready to cast their spells on anyone walking softly and not carrying a stick.

It's said that Joan of Arc used to make her warriors get down on their knees, confess their sins, and cleanse their souls before going into battle. Maybe she knew intuitively that any lingering, unresolved guilt would muck up the soul and weaken a warrior's power.

In Aikido, students learn the art of sending negative energy back to the sender. It is an art based on nonresistance. Strength and speed are not considered power. Students learn to stay alert and focused—not paranoid—watching in front of and behind themselves.

I felt confused at first—and for a while—when I began studying Aikido. Each time my teacher or another student made a move on me in training, I would look at my teacher and say, "What should I do? I don't know what to do."

My teacher wouldn't respond. He believes that students learn best by struggling through the confusion and figuring things out themselves. I would be twisted, pulled, pushed, yanked, and sometimes punched. And I would just stand there. After months of passively allowing myself to be mauled, I caught on.

"I finally figured out what to do when someone tries to punch me," I said to my teacher one day.

"What?" he asked.

"Duck," I said.

Back in the sandlot, Essam asked me what I wanted to do that day. To my surprise, I decided to go horseback riding. I had never ridden a horse before in my life. Once, when I was about three, a relative had placed me on top of a horse. That stallion looked so big. I immediately toppled off. The fall knocked the wind out of me, in that painful way that happens when you take a sudden, unexpected blow to the solar plexus. A group of relatives stood around laughing, watching me roll on the ground groaning and trying desperately not to cry. I never mounted a horse again, except the beautiful, carved, wooden ones on the merry-go-round at the fair.

Now, I swung my leg over the side of this horse and mounted it as if I had been riding all my life. The saddle was layers of old blankets tied around the horse's back. Essam's nephew, the young man who had accompanied me to the pyramids, rode next to me again. We started at a slow trot, precariously scaling the rocky hills. When we reached the flat expanse of the desert, we both began galloping through the dust. I leaned forward, riding that horse as fast as he would go. The February air blew cool against my face.

I felt powerful and free.

After an hour or so, we came to a pile of rocks and dismounted. I sat in the sand, leaning against the rocks, drinking from the bottle of water I had stashed in my backpack.

"Do you have a husband?" the young man asked.

"Not anymore," I said. "I'm divorced."

"You ought to come to Egypt and live," he said. "You could have more than one husband here."

I gave him a strange look. "Women can have more than one husband here?" I asked.

"Oh, yes," he said.

"What about the men? Do they get more than one wife?"

"Yes," the young man said.

"I think you've got that confused," I said. "You're telling me that women get more than one husband, men get more than one wife, and everyone is able to make sense out of that and live happily?"

The young man smiled. "Yes. You should come here. You'd like it."

I laughed.

"I probably would," I said.

We got back on our horses and returned to the perfume shop.

Essam had lunch waiting for me. He didn't eat; it was Ramadan and still daylight. We sat on the bench outside the shop talking while I ate. I was so hungry I felt only slightly guilty about eating in front of him.

When I finished eating, I looked around for a restroom. I didn't see one in the store. Essam said there was none in the shop, that tourists usually went somewhere in the village to use facilities. Then he said I was more than welcome to go to his home, which was next door, and use the bathroom there.

I followed him around the store, through a court-yard littered with children's toys, to the door of a sprawling one-story home. It looked new and fairly modern. Essam told me that in the village of Giza his house was considered a mansion. He lived there with his aunt, his sisters, his brother-in-law, and their children. He told me to go in, turn to the right and I would come to the bathroom. I walked into a maze of rooms, then found a series of rooms each of which seemed like part of the bathroom. The first tiny room contained a sink. I wasn't sure if the water worked or not. In the next room, a faucet projected out of the wall. I guessed that was the shower. In the next room was a toilet. Next to it was a large basin of water and a wooden ladle for flushing.

When I exited the bathroom and walked back through the house, I inadvertently turned the wrong way. Suddenly I was standing in the midst of a room of women. They were sitting on the floor on layers of rugs and pillows, watching television. They wore long, colorful dresses. I smiled. One woman, the woman in the middle, motioned for me to sit down next to her.

I did.

They didn't speak English. I didn't speak Arabic. So we just sat there. Their eyes glowed. They seemed so happy to have company. I got a little nervous after a while. I didn't know what to do next, and they didn't want me to leave. Finally, Essam entered the room.

He talked to them for a minute, then turned to me.

"They like you," he said.

When we returned to the bench on the sandlot, I told Essam what his nephew had told me and asked him if it was true that women were allowed to marry more than one husband.

Essam shook his head. "No," he said. "That is not true. Women are allowed one husband. Men can take four wives."

"What about divorce?" I asked. "Can a woman divorce her husband if she's unhappy or they have serious problems?"

Essam shook his head again. "No. The woman cannot divorce her husband. Only the husband can divorce the wife."

"That's not fair," I said. "It doesn't sound like a good deal to me."

A heavy pause filled the air.

"It is not a good thing to be born a woman in this country," Essam finally said. "It starts at birth. Everyone gathers around waiting to hear whether the child born is a male or a female. If they come out and say it is a boy, fireworks! The people scream and cheer. They celebrate—sometimes for days! But if they come out and say it's a girl, there is silence. No one says a word. The people act like they heard nothing. They turn, walk away, and return to what they were doing."

As I listened to Essam tell me about Egyptian women, I again felt a faint stirring within me, as I had outside the pyramids my first night in Cairo. For much of my life, I had quietly raged about being a woman and about the inequality in power, not just between the sexes but between people. It seemed to me that so often, certain people of title, role, and sex were naturally afforded power—it was an entitlement of sorts—while others had to work so hard for this same power, often even to convince others or themselves that they *had* power. I had raged, albeit silently, about the constraints I felt—the expectations, the limitations, and the constant need to prove my power—power automatically bestowed on some whether or not that presumption of power was warranted.

Sitting in the sandlot, I began to see that some of our beliefs about power are prefabricated, doled and rationed out to us in our youth, sometimes at the moment of birth, sometimes before we're born. So are many of our limitations—like not being able to ride a horse.

I was getting tired of presuming others had power and I had none.

I wondered how deep, and how ancient, my rage really was.

It had taken me many years to understand that I had power. It had taken me even longer to begin to understand how to use it. Often I became confused about what power I had in any situation and what power I didn't have. When my son died, I felt so impotent that I forgot I had any power at all. When the doctor told me there was no hope, I swallowed my rage and bitterly accepted my powerlessness. There was nothing I could do.

I had set down my stick and walked away from it. I had forgotten I had a stick.

By now, back at the sandlot, the sun was almost ready to set. I told Essam I was tired. It had been a long day; I was ready to return to the hotel. He talked about things I could do the next time I visited.

"Usually the women do not mingle with the tourists," he said. "But they really like you. They asked that you come back for dinner or at least dessert. They want to see you again." He scanned my attire. I was wearing a dark sweat suit. "I want to get you a dress," he said. "With your dark hair and dark skin, I could then take you into the village. People will think you are from here. There are many things for you to do," he said. "And soon you will be ready to go inside the pyramids and meditate. Then you will get the special powers."

I felt excited, curious, and honored to meet the women. I didn't understand what Essam meant about "getting the special powers" from the pyramids. But as I sat on the bench outside Lotus Palace Perfumes remembering how I had felt riding that horse across the desert, I knew I had unearthed and resurrected my power.

A boy was riding a donkey around the sandlot. In his hand, he held a stick—a shorter model of the one I had seen the night before in the *souk.*

I told Essam I would be happy to do all the things he discussed, then I pointed to the stick in the boy's hand.

"But I want one of those, too," I said, "to help me remember."

Essam smiled. He didn't say anything. I knew he understood. I finally understood, too. I didn't need to *buy* a stick. I already had one. Each of us does. All we need to do is pick it up and use it.

Scheherazade, the mythical heroine of the Arabian Nights, *put her stick to good use. She lived in a land where the sultan—the king—had been deeply betrayed by his wife. (One day, the sultan had returned home unexpectedly from a journey and found his beloved cavorting with another.) To deal with his broken heart, he had had that wife beheaded. Then, to ensure that no woman would ever again betray him, he had mandated that each night he would take a new wife, a virgin. After sleeping with her one night, he would have her beheaded when she arose the next morning.*

This had gone on for years. Mothers in the land were weeping, either in grief from losing their daughter or in fear that their female child would be next. Scheherazade went to her father, a consult to the sultan. She asked her father to give her to the sultan so she could be the sultan's next wife. Her father recoiled in horror, but Scheherazade insisted. She said something must be done, and she was the one to do it.

She said she had a plan.

For the next one thousand and one nights, Scheherazade enraptured the sultan with her storytelling skills. Each night, she told the sultan a portion of a story, taking it to its most engaging point. Then she would suddenly stop, asking the sultan for permission to continue the story the next day. The sultan of course agreed. Scheherazade's stories were marvelous tales about oppressed, middle-class people who used their wills, wiles, artistic skills, and faith in Allah to fulfill their destinies and desires in the most magical ways. Scheherazade's storytelling skills were so artful the sultan could barely wait to hear the rest of each story. To behead her was unthinkable. On the nights she finished a story, Scheherazade would simply say, "But that story is no more strange or wondrous than the one I am about to tell you next."

By the time she finished telling all her stories, she had given the sultan three children and he had fallen in love with her. He repented of his hatred toward women, deciding not all of them were evil. He made amends to the people of his land, the best that he could, for the harm that he had done. Scheherazade saved the women of her country. She healed the sultan's heart. And her wonderful tales taught millions of people how powerful they and Allah were.

Scheherazade didn't let anyone tell her how much power she had. She knew how powerful she was. She had learned a most important secret about life and about power. She didn't dwell on the power she didn't have. She mastered the art of working with the power she knew was hers.

Scheherazade picked up her stick, then used it masterfully, with flair.

I STILL DO NOT UNDERSTAND what the women in Egypt could possibly have to do with the women in your country," the interrogator said, whipping me back to the airport in Tel Aviv. "These women have no freedom. They do not even leave their homes."

Ah, I thought. Now you're beginning to understand codependency . . .

I leaned forward on the desk, letting it brace me for support. By now my back ached and my voice was scratchy. "I write to women and to men," I said. "And you are right. I live in a wonderful country. My people have many freedoms, freedoms and luxuries unknown in some parts of the world. But many people in my country do not understand how free they are," I responded.

"Take me, for example," I said. "For ten years, I was locked in a box . . ."

chapter 8

Locked in the Box

Sunset was the sacred signal that broke the daily fast. At dusk, the quiet village of Giza came to life. This day was no exception. The men and boys scurried about the sandlot with a vitality obscured during daylight hours by hunger and the sheer strain of abstinence. Three camels knelt on the far end of the lot, smiling mysteriously as if they possessed a secret unknown to any other creature or being.

I followed Essam past the perfume shop and down the dirt path leading to his home. In his hand he held a white cardboard box of treasured delicacies from the village bakery—half a dozen lemon bars made with flaky, golden pastry and a dozen date-filled Egyptian cookies.

We had already eaten a scrumptious meal. Now we were going to his house to eat dessert and take tea with the women.

"So how old are the women when they get locked in the box?" I asked.

Essam stopped short.

"The box?" he asked.

"Yes," I said. "How old are they when they have to get in the box?" I pointed to the house.

He smiled in recognition. "Oh, you mean when do they have to begin staying at home."

I nodded.

"When a girl turns fourteen, she is expected to stay at home. It is the women's job to cook, clean, and raise the children," he said.

"Do they have to stay in the house for the rest of their lives?" I asked.

He nodded.

"Are they *ever* allowed out?"

"Sometimes to go to market," he said.

"How boring," I said. "I hope you put music in the box to make it better for them."

Essam looked at me as if he didn't completely understand. How would this gentle man understand? I thought. He's not been locked in the box.

He held the door open for me. I entered, then waited to follow his lead. We walked through the room where I had first met the women, the room with all the rugs and pillows on the floor. He led me around the corner to the left, into a more formal living room. This room was small. It contained a sofa, a chair, and an end table.

Two of the women I had met yesterday stood waiting to greet me. Essam introduced me to the older of the women, his aunt, and the younger woman, his sister. The women looked frail and tired. His aunt looked especially weary. Essam's nephew, a thin, fair-haired boy about nine years old, sat on the sofa amidst school books and papers. He clutched the nub of a pencil in his hand and sat poring over his homework. With the shyness of a young boy, he barely looked at me when we were introduced. Later I saw him peeking. A vibrant teenage girl with blazing eyes and shiny dark hair walked boldly up to me. She held my hand in a warm hello that didn't need words. She was stunningly beautiful. Her radiance instantly reminded me of my daughter, Nichole.

No one in the room spoke English except for Essam, so he translated for us. The teenage girl was his niece. She was seventeen and very glad to meet me. All the women were honored to have me in their home.

I told them I was pleased and honored to be there.

The two women sat on the floor. One lit the flame on a small stove that looked like a camping stove, then began boiling water for tea. Essam gestured for me to sit next to his nephew on the small sofa, which I did. His niece immediately squeezed in next to me on the other side.

Essam opened the box of pastries and began passing them around. His nephew, after much urging, took a lemon bar out of the white box and began munching on it. His niece held my hand in hers, touching my painted nails. The women peered at me, refusing any dessert. And the faint stirring I had felt so many times here in this ancient village now turned into a whirling maelstrom taking me someplace far back in time.

The year was 1975. I was twenty-eight years old, a newlywed, eager to explore my dreams of being a wife and mother. Slowly over the ensuing months and years, a combination of forces made it harshly clear that my dreams were fantasies—mere illusions. By then, I had two children. I loved them deeply. I loved being their mother. But poverty, my husband's alcoholism, and my response to his alcoholism—which I would later label codependency—had slowly ground me down to almost nothing. Although there were years when I had no car, no telephone, and little food, money was the least of what I lacked. I had no self, no self-identity, and no life. I had become embittered, drained, and weary. I rarely left the house. I had little contact with people. I had even less contact with myself—my emotions, thoughts, or power. I spun off other people's expectations of me, or what I believed they expected. I no longer knew what I wanted from life, and I certainly didn't expect much from myself or from anyone else.

I was locked in a box.

I had been in boxes before. As a child, I had felt miserably trapped. At age twelve I began crossing off days on the calendar, counting to the hour how much time I had to put in before I would be set free. My release date was age eighteen. I had few choices then, except to wait for the passage of time. I did just that. But in the process of waiting for my freedom, I turned my rage and bitterness against myself.

By the time I was let out of that childhood box, I had already put myself in another—I was addicted to alcohol and drugs. Then, after getting out of that trap, I walked smack into another box. I found myself married to an alcoholic and locked into my futile attempts to make him stop drinking. I told myself I had no choices then. There didn't seem to be any way out.

Over the years, I gradually began to understand some things about codependency and about my self-nullifying response to other people. I found an old Royal typewriter, one with the "n" key missing. I began communicating with the world around me by telling my stories. I also began communicating with myself. I found a way out of that box, a way out for my children and me. That would not be the last box I'd walk into, but it was the last time I would believe I was trapped.

Many situations and circumstances in life can box us in with expectations that are not ours, limitations that diminish our freedom and dim the light in our golden ball of power. It's so easy to allow others to infringe on our lives, wishes, emotions, and choices. The edges protecting free will are thin.

I had been working for years to break out of all the obvious boxes. But at each new level, the boxes—the traps—became more subtle. Slowly I began to see that many of the boxes I found myself in were of my own making. I tended to construct them, crawl in, then wonder who I could blame for putting me there. Who did this to me? I would wonder and sometimes ask aloud. That's when I'd hear the answer: *You did,* Melody. You put yourself in this box. *Now it's up to you to get out.*

There are enough situations in life we can't change, control, or do anything about. We don't need to complicate an already intricate and complex life by limiting our choices and putting ourselves in a box.

Yet, over the years, that's what I had done.

Recently, I had begun to suspect that some deep part of me reveled, at least for a while, in the safety and comfort of being confined, limited, and controlled. I had also begun to suspect that what Nelson Mandela and others have said is true. It is not our darkness, our capability to create mayhem and madness, that we fear. What frightens us is our greatness and our tremendous inherent potential for brilliance.

Now, sitting in the living room in Essam's mansion in the village of Giza, I felt all the emotions that accompany being locked in the box—a deep, burning rage and bitterness, fatigue, weariness, hopelessness, and such a strong aversion to confinement that I could barely sit still. I took a bite of my delicious lemon bar, wondering how deep and ancient these emotional memories were.

I really didn't like being locked in a box.

Essam's niece handed me a family photo album. I leafed through the pictures. Not speaking the language made visiting difficult. Small talk normally fills many silent voids, but when small talk has to be translated it's often not worth mentioning. I sipped my tea. Suddenly, I couldn't restrain myself anymore.

I turned to Essam's niece. "Tell her, Essam. Tell her she doesn't have to stay in the box."

His eyes got wide.

"Tell her," I said. "She's beautiful. She radiates life. She could do anything, be anything she wants . . ."

Essam smiled, then began translating my words into Arabic. His niece listened intently, then her radiant face glowed more brightly. She wanted to hear more.

"You could be a model," I said. "A movie star. Work in an office. You don't have to stay in the box all your life. I have a daughter. She's your age. She's beautiful too. She's on the cutting edge of her life. So are you. Live it!"

Essam translated. The young girl smiled. I could have talked all night. A fleeting thought crossed my mind, quieting my voice: an Arab nation under

Islamic rule is not the place to do a *Codependent No More* tour.

I was crossing that invisible yet real line between helping and becoming excessively involved in affairs that weren't mine. I could feel it. I remembered the words my friend's daughter had written on her hand as a reminder not to become entangled in a girl-friend's romantic dilemma: "DON'T HELP." I didn't have to control the world. There was a greater plan. This plan could be trusted. I didn't have to *make* anything happen. I could *let* destiny evolve.

I sat back on the sofa. "Please pass the lemon bars," I said to Essam.

We sat in the living room drinking tea, conversing the best that we could. After a while, Essam stood up. "The women have a gift for you," he said. "Please come with me."

I followed him into a room that looked like a dining room, except there was no table in it. Framed photos of men in military uniforms covered one long wall. I stared at the pictures while I waited for the women. Soon they entered the room carrying arm-fuls of long gowns, each in a solid, vibrant color—red, yellow, purple, green, blue, white.

"They want you to choose two dresses," Essam said. "It's a gift from them."

I held each dress up in front of me, one at a time, trying to decide which two looked best on me. They were all so beautiful.

"They want you to try them on," Essam translated. "They want to see what you look like in an Egyptian gown."

Essam left the room. I modeled each of the exotic, beautiful dresses for the women. We oohed, aahed, and giggled. Finally, after much debate and several repeat performances, we decided that the scarlet dress with the sequined star and the peacock green dress were the right ones for me.

I thanked the women. Essam's sister patted my arm. His aunt smiled. It was the first time I had seen her smile all night.

Essam came back into the room. I showed him the dresses I had chosen. Then his aunt took my arm, guiding me to the wall with the photos. She pointed to a picture of a dashing man dressed in full military garb.

"She wants you to know that's her husband," Essam said. "He was killed in the war."

I looked at Essam's aunt. That's what I had sensed in her—that deep grief from losing someone we love. I looked at her, wishing I could do something for her. She has lost so much, I thought. Essam then told her I had lost my son. She touched her hand to her chest, the universal sign communicating that a person understands a broken heart.

Essam translated, and his aunt and I talked for a while about grief and about death. We had something in common. We both felt betrayed by life. Then Essam asked if I was ready to go. I said yes.

"Tell them thank you very much," I said. "I had a wonderful evening."

Essam and the women talked in Arabic for a while, then Essam turned to me. "They enjoyed your visit very much," he said. "They are sad you have to go. They want you to come back soon."

"Tell them I will," I said. "I promise."

That's when Essam taught me the meaning of *Insha'a Allah.*

"Never say 'I will do this' or 'I will do that,'" Essam said. "Instead say, 'I will do that *Insha'a Allah.'*"

"What does that mean?" I asked.

"If God wills it," he said.

"Then tell them I will be back *Insha'a Allah.*"

He smiled.

I walked out the front door of the house. I intended to return soon, but this would be the last time, at least on this trip, that I would see these lovely women of Giza.

Essam and I walked to a restaurant in the downtown area of the village. He directed me to a small outdoor table at the restaurant, then ordered tea for us. I ran across the street to an open-air market to get some tangerines.

"Take off your shoes," Essam said when I returned to the table.

"What?" I asked, wondering what kind of cultural tradition this was.

"Take off your shoes," he said again.

I noticed how dusty my walking boots were as I unlaced and removed them. Essam knelt down, took my boots in his hand, stood up, smiled, then pointed to a shop across the street.

"I'm getting your shoes shined," he said. "They're covered with the desert."

Shortly, Essam returned to the table with my shoes. We sat drinking tea and talking about the tangerines, the village, and my plans for the rest of the week. I was considering moving from the large hotel in Cairo to a smaller hotel on the edge of Giza. I hadn't yet begun writing. This concerned me, but there were so many things to see and do, so many people to meet. These adventures felt so important.

"I have some more family members I would like you to meet," Essam said.

"Who?" I asked.

"There are about five thousand of them," he said.

I laughed. Then Essam's mood shifted visibly.

"I had to divorce my wife, Melody," he said after a long pause.

"Why?" I asked.

"Because she wouldn't stay in the box," he said.

His voice was tinted with sadness, his face and eyes clouded with confusion. In that moment, in that look in his face, I saw so many things.

Men need women as much as or more than women need men, I thought, whether that need expresses itself as a need for friendship or a romantic relationship. I looked around at the streets devoid of the presence of women, as many of the streets in the Arab world had been except in the *souk*. Societies need the balance brought by female energy, I thought. That's what's missing here. To be complete and live in a way that brings us into harmony with ourselves and the world, we *each* need the daily presence and involvement of the feminine side of ourselves—our intuition, nurturing, creativity.

Essam was strong, yet he was a kind, gentle man. In all my time here, I had seen him wield power over no one. He seemed to accept and enjoy my independence and freedom, even though I'm a woman. I wondered why allowing his wife freedom threatened him so much. Could it be that even though men appeared to have so much more power than women, men perceived women as actually being more powerful than men? Did they look at women with the same illusions about power that women sometimes had when they saw men? Was this whole dance a big power play, where people suffered from the illusion they didn't have power and then tried to repress the power in others—steal power—to try to bring things into balance?

The world is changing, I thought. Our world in the United States—even this world here in the Middle East—is changing. One person can no longer have power by denying another his or her freedom or power. The world is bringing itself—and the male and female energies in it—into balance.

Taking power from another no longer works. Power—whether it is emotional, spiritual, mental, physical, psychic, or financial—is a tremendous responsibility. The Golden Rule—do unto others as you would have them do unto you—is not a suggestion. It's a law that decodes how the universe works. How we use our powers, how we behave, how we treat others boomerangs back to us. Even the subtle ways we direct our thoughts, emotions, and intentions toward others will inevitably come back to haunt us, particularly when we intermingle these powerful energies with our will.

Ultimately, how we love our neighbor *is* how we love and treat ourselves.

Years ago, I practiced the ritual of praying for people I resented. I hadn't understood the rationale for doing this. I did it because people I trusted told me to. They told me that it was better than seeking revenge and that praying for people I resented worked—which it did. I had done this on blind faith. Now, I began to see *why* it worked. When we seek revenge, we are really targeting that spiteful energy at ourselves. When we project mean energy, it can and will be turned back on us. It's inevitable. It has to go somewhere. And when we pray for another—even if we have to force the words until they feel real—we're really praying for blessings to be heaped upon ourselves. We're projecting an energy that is desirable to have redirected and turned back at us.

Make no mistake, there is a vast difference between a reckoning and revenge.

In Aikido, I learned that the art's powerful defense techniques were effective only if someone attacked. If a person did not attack, there was no negative energy—no force—to direct back at that person.

I pestered my sensei for a book I could read, some-thing that would help me to mentally configure the ideas I was struggling so hard to learn. I wanted to understand in my head how to work with energy that was directed at me, how to intuitively, immediately, and gracefully send all negative energy back to its source in the dojo and in my life. I wanted the recipe for how to protect myself without becoming vengeful, aggressive, or overly hurtful. I wanted to learn everything I could about power, because it was setting me free. And I wanted a list of rules, an instruction booklet to help me do that.

"That's not how you learn," my teacher said. "Struggle through the confusion until your body, mind, and spirit learn how it feels when you get it right. Then you'll really know. And then you'll remember."

"But there must be something I can read," I protested.

Finally, on my own, I found a book that discussed these ideas, a book called The Art of War. *When I told my teacher about the book, he said it was a good one. "But when you finish that, there's a better one," he said. "It's called* The Art of Peace.*"*

Back in Giza, as I sat in the outdoor restaurant drinking my tea, talking to Essam, and thinking about power, women, and revenge, I noticed a young boy riding a donkey bareback down the street. This ancient village mesmerized me. It was a journey back in time.

"Look!" I said to Essam, pointing at the animal.

"Do you want to ride it?" Essam asked.

I hesitated. Essam insisted. He called to the boy. Then we walked over to the donkey. The boy dismounted. I swung my leg over the back of the animal, hoisted myself up, then rode that ass bareback down the street.

It had taken me a long time, but I was out of the box. And I had no intention of getting back in *Insha'a Allah*.

L ET ME SEE YOUR NOTES," the female interrogator with the chestnut-colored hair demanded, reeling me back into the airport in Tel Aviv.

I recoiled in disbelief. I felt invaded and violated. Didn't I have any rights? What was this woman looking for? What did she think I had found?

"I want to see your notes," she repeated firmly. "Anything at all you have written that pertains to this book."

My hands shook as I fished through my suitcase and dug out my file.

"I don't have a lot," I said, handing her some papers. "But here they are."

"Read them to me, please," she said.

I put on my glasses, then struggled to read my almost illegible writing.

"*Stop Being Mean to Yourself* is about a journey into self-love. It's about having compassion for others. But it's about learning to have compassion for ourselves, too."

I paused. "Oh," I said. "At the bottom of the page I have one more thing scrawled."

She looked at me, waiting.

"It's an awfully big adventure . . ."

chapter 9

Finding the Key

Before the birth of written language, ancient civilizations documented and preserved important communications and messages by carving pictures and symbols in stone. These pictures and symbols expressed ideas rather than words, as writing does now.

Although Egypt graduated from etching symbols in stone to writing on papyrus almost five thousand years ago, much

Egyptian art still consists of symbolic one-dimensional drawings. These pictures are not just intended to capture a particular scene as the artist saw, interpreted, and then rendered it. They are symbolic pictures—sacred art meant to communicate a specific message or story directly to a person's heart and mind.

On this day, in Giza, Essam and I went shopping in the village. I needed a few incidentals—some fruit, a music tape, some aspirin. I had also been instructed to buy four white candles to bring into the pyramids with me while I meditated. When I finished shopping, Essam took me to meet another of his relatives, a doctor who is also a perfume merchant. We took tea with the doctor and visited for a while. Almost abruptly, Essam stood up.

"Please come with me now," he said. "It is time for you to get your pictures."

I didn't understand what he was talking about, but by now I trusted Essam. He had become more than a friend. He had become a teacher and a guide for this part of my Arabian expedition.

I had no idea, as I followed him to the car, that today would hold a key to a mystery I'd been trying to unravel for years.

I have spent a fair degree of time in my life looking for keys—car keys, house keys, garage keys. Keys.

I have spent more time looking for one key in particular—the key to the mystery of life.

It was as if there was a big locked metal door. On one side of it was pure, true edification and wisdom, supreme knowledge of why we're here and how to be happy and fulfilled while we're here—enlightenment.

I, however, was on the other side, locked out, spinning my wheels, futilely searching for the key.

Over the years, I had been to therapists, doctors, and healers. I had used homeopathy, kinesiology, acupuncture, and acupressure. I read books and had written some of my own. I regularly searched through magazines, clipping out articles, looking for clues to the key. I had attended workshops. I talked to people. I talked to God. I practiced the tenets of the faith I was raised in, and believed in—Christianity. Then, I exposed myself to the other great religions of the world.

In my youth I had tried alcohol and drugs, thinking they were the answer. I had used and abused LSD, cocaine, heroin, and morphine. I ingested marijuana, alcohol, barbiturates, and amphetamines looking for the answer in mind-altering, chemically induced spiritual experiences.

Later, I looked for the answer in relationships. Then, I thought possibly the answer was to avoid romantic relationships.

I tried Gestalt therapy, Transactional Analysis, hypnotherapy, prayer, and meditation. And over the last twenty-three years, I had been an active participant in more than one twelve-step program.

I used affirmations. I listened to tapes. I felt my feelings. I monitored my thought process. I served others obsessively. Then I redefined service, so that I was serving joyfully, rather than compulsively. I struggled to love myself. I learned to be assertive. I dealt with my glaring codependency issues, my sense of nonexistent self and my clinging-vine dependency.

I then marched dutifully forward into the grinding work so many people have come to love and know as family-of-origin work. I began the grueling and eternal process of detoxifying—or healing—my repressed and embedded emotional blocks and correlating limiting beliefs, these so-called barriers to wisdom, fulfillment, and enlightenment that I had accumulated since time immemorial. Hooray, I finally found and healed my inner child. I nurtured her. I loved her the best I could. I even had a fuzzy teddy bear, God bless John Bradshaw, stashed in the closet in my library.

I connected with and learned to take care of my body, understanding its intricate connection to the soul. I was on estrogen therapy for hormone replacement and vitamin therapy for nutritional support.

After my son died, I stayed with my grief, every gut-wrenching, heart-breaking, mind-shattering moment of it. Then I worked through my grief, finally accepting the lifetime handicap of the loss of my son.

I went on to peruse the Course in Miracles, *where I learned with Marianne Williamson's help about the magic of love in all its myriad shapes and forms, diligently remembering that love also included saying "no" and sometimes "get away."*

At last, I opened my heart.

Then, climbing the ladder of spiritual growth, I put my foot on the next rung. With the rest of the nation, I read, spellbound, Betty Eadie's Embraced by the Light, *awestruck by the mystery of life after death.*

I loved that book. But I still didn't understand the mystery of life before death.

I was still looking for that key.

Over the years, as a result of my search, my values had changed. Whereas I used to fantasize about gold and diamonds, I now accumulated and treasured beautiful rocks—lapis lazuli, shimmering crystals from the Himalayas, amethyst, rose quartz, watermelon tourmaline. These were now my precious gems. I used oils and aromatherapy. I chose my colors carefully. I avoided polyester like the plague.

But sometimes, in the middle of the night, I still wondered, should I just give in, join the rest of the world, and start taking Prozac?

I knew I wasn't alone in my search. Most of the people I knew were on a similar quest. They were looking for the key. Some purported to have it, but they charged so much for their seminars I wasn't willing to attend.

The year before this trip to the Middle East, I spent three months traveling to sacred sites around the western United States. I soaked in some of the most potent, healing, mineral-laden hot springs in this country. I visited the vortexes of Sedona, the ancient Anasazi village in Chaco Canyon, and the blessed New Mexican church, the Sanctuario de Chimayo. I gazed upon rocks and ruins and waterfalls and rain forests, absorbing that energy into my soul.

I should have been glowing in the damn dark.

It felt as if I was in a tunnel. Occasionally, I would get glimpses of light. But in those moments I felt more blinded than I did embraced by it. Most of the time, I couldn't see what I was doing or where I was going. I didn't understand what this entire excursion was all about.

Many of the therapies, people, ideas, and resources I stumbled onto over the years had genuinely helped.

While some endeavors were feel good activities (they felt good while I was doing them but didn't affect me that greatly overall) and a few schemes, such as using drugs, had impaired me (I had to later spend time and money undoing the damage I had done to myself), most of these undertakings had caused a permanent, beneficial change in me and in my life.

But I still couldn't find the key.

I couldn't unlock the door and get in that room.

I couldn't find enlightenment.

Sometimes I'd think I'm almost there, I'm on the edge of it, I'm so close to a breakthrough I can feel it. Then I'd make a run at that door and bam! I'd crash headlong into it and fall in a crumpled heap on the floor. The door was still locked. At least it appeared to be. On the other side, a few feet away, just out of reach, were the treasures I sought. But I couldn't quite get to them.

I wasn't necessarily depressed, but my spirit ached. Sometimes it was a dull, agitating pain. Other times, it was closer to anguish. I was so grindingly dissatisfied. Life could be so disappointing. Here we were, approaching the millennium, this glorious, exhilarating time that so many people were buzzing about. But it didn't feel all that spine-tingling to me. It felt confusing and at times debilitating. I didn't get it. I didn't get the millennium—at least not what it meant personally to me and the people I knew. I didn't get what this entire undertaking was all about. I didn't get enlightenment.

At times it seemed like the harder I worked to gain understanding, the less I understood.

Maybe tomorrow, I'd think. Maybe tomorrow I'll find that key. It seemed as if enlightenment was always one day, one step, one therapist, one book, one healer, one something away—no matter what I did. I was becoming weary and skeptical.

I wondered. Was I engaged in a legitimate truth-seeking expedition that was leading somewhere? Or were all these activities mere busy work, an experiment in futility, some sort of punitive endurance test on a cosmic treadmill?

Over fifteen years ago, when I was already well immersed in this quest, a trusted friend told me that the secret to life was simple: there was no secret. That didn't sound right to me. There must be one, I thought. I knew there was a key, although it promised to remain eternally out of my reach. Now, after all these years of searching, I was beginning to wonder. Maybe my friend was right. Maybe I was looking for something that didn't exist.

This day in Giza, I would find the key to unlock that door.

Essam hailed a taxi, and we wove through the streets of Giza plaza, making our way to a small shop located behind a hospital. We were in a part of the city I had not yet seen. The sign in the shop's window announced that we were at Nile River Papyrus. Essam told the driver to wait for him, then he escorted me inside. It was a tiny, narrow store. Almost every square inch of the walls was covered with Egyptian art that had been hand-painted on papyrus.

"I will leave you here for one hour," Essam said. "Look around. See if any of the pictures speak to you. Remember, if you find any pictures you like, do not pay the marked price. Half, and no more. I will tell the shopkeeper that, too."

After speaking for a while in Arabic to the man behind the counter, Essam left. The papyrus merchant, a thin man who appeared to be in his early twenties, asked if I would like to see a demonstration of how papyrus was made. I told him I would. So he began to tell and show me the story of this ancient art.

In a land where few trees grow, the papyrus plant flourishes. About forty-six hundred years ago, ancient Egyptians discovered that if they cut the inner portion of the papyrus stalk into razor-thin strips and soaked these strips in water, the strips could then be woven into flat sheets. After pressing and drying the sheets under something heavy, like a rock, the Egyptians could then make the same markings on these sheets that they had been, until now, dutifully carving in stone. Unlike rocks, these sheets could be rolled, stored, and easily transported. The ancient Egyptian civilization had stumbled onto a way to record, preserve, and disseminate ideas and information. Lighter than stone, papyrus paper revolutionized their world.

The shopkeeper showed me how the thin strips of pith, the inner portion of the stalk or reed, were sliced, soaked, then woven into a flat sheet. He showed me how the woven sheets were pressed and dried. Then he showed me the finished product—the ivory-yellow parchment-like sheets called papyrus. He explained that papyrus can be drawn or written on using oil colors, water colors, coal, ink, a typewriter, or gouache (a form of water-color paint). He showed me how easily the sheets can be rolled and stored in a cylinder.

"Go ahead. Look around," he said, when he finished his demonstration. "See if you like any of our pictures."

I walked to the far end of the store. Vibrantly colored pictures of all sizes covered the walls. The pictures were vastly different from the art I was used to looking at—art that expressed an artist's rendition of a particular scene or a portrait. These pictures were simple one-dimensional drawings, but they were hauntingly profound. Many of the pictures were implanted with hieroglyphic symbols. Because of the large number of drawings and the difference in this art form, it took me a while to focus.

Gradually, I shifted from looking at everything at once to studying the individual pictures. I saw many drawings of the pyramids and the Sphinx. I noticed an intricate astrological wheel with ancient Egyptian symbols. It was beautiful, but when I studied it, I thought about a friend of mine. It didn't really speak to me. I continued to look. Soon, I saw my first picture.

It was a simple drawing of the Virgin Mary holding the Christ child in her arms.

Mary wore a flowing blue gown. A golden halo encircled her head. The blue in her gown was of an indescribable shade and hue. The child she held was barefoot. A golden halo encircled his head too. Both of them wore golden crowns.

I wasn't now and had never been a member of the Catholic church, but Mary had become increasingly important to me over the past years. Her gentle spirit, tender ways, and magnificent healing power had helped my heart to heal in a time when little else could touch me.

She has the lightness and love of the angels and the healing power of her Son.

Her energy calms and soothes me, yet sometimes takes my breath away.

I feel completely and utterly safe when I am in her presence.

I feel quietly empowered, confident, and strengthened.

I also feel understood.

She is the feminine side of the Divine.

This picture spoke to me.

"I want that one," I said.

The young man took the picture of Mary and the Christ child off the wall and placed it on the counter. I continued to look around. Soon, another picture attracted my interest. It was an intricate weaving of people, hieroglyphics, and animal-like creatures. It was long and narrow, about five feet wide and two feet high. I liked it but I didn't understand it, so I moved on. Something about this picture pulled me back. Noticing my interest, the merchant began telling me its story.

"This picture represents Egyptian mythology about life after death and how one enters Paradise," he said. "When you die, you go before a council. At that time, your heart is removed and placed on one of the pans of a balancing scale. A feather is placed in the other pan. If your heart weighs the same as or less than a feather, you are allowed to enter Paradise. If not," he said, scowling and shaking his head, "your heart is fed to the dragons."

I studied the long, narrow drawing. Now that he had explained the story, I could see it clearly. All four scenes were there: a figure sitting before the council, this same figure standing next to the balancing scales, this figure being led to a door, and finally the ornate room representing paradise.

For thousands of years, this ancient culture had known what it had taken me most of my life to understand.

When I was twelve years old, I already had a burgeoning problem with alcohol. From the first time I sneaked a drink from the bottle of Jack Daniels stashed in the back of the cupboard underneath the kitchen sink, I had a problem—although I didn't see it as a problem at the time. All I could see was that I loved the warm tingling glow as the fiery juice slipped down my throat and kicked into my stomach.

It felt good.

This particular summer, I was headed to a Baptist Bible camp in northern Minnesota. I had attended this camp before. These people were serious; they meant business; it was more Bible than camp. But this summer I would be prepared. I carefully filled seven tiny perfume bottles—one for each day of the week—with whiskey. Then I tucked the bottles into my rolled-up socks and carefully stashed them in my suitcase.

I breezed through the first two days of camp. I had to attend, as all participants did, many church services and lectures. But I also had the comfort of the sun, the fresh air, the lake, the boats, the swimming—and my seven perfume bottles filled with Jack Daniels. On the third day of camp, while I was dutifully building a Popsicle-stick house during arts and crafts, two senior camp counselors approached me. They hovered over me, giving me **that look**. Then, they showed me the perfume bottles they had confiscated from my room. I instantly knew the party was over.

The counselors marched me to a sink and forced me to watch while they poured my whiskey down the drain. Then they led me into a small room, a room way too small for three people to be in I thought at the time. We sat in a circle on metal folding chairs. With great solemnity, the counselors informed me that they were extremely disappointed in me. That wasn't news. I was extremely disappointed in myself, too. I had been for a long time. Then they gave me the Coming to Jesus Option. They felt, they said, obligated to tele-

phone my mother immediately and inform her of this serious and flagrant violation of camp rules. However, they also saw fit to give me a loophole. If I were willing to march to the altar during a special church service—in front of all my junior-high peers—get down on my knees, confess my sins, and let Jesus come into my heart, they wouldn't feel quite so obligated to call my mother.

"Okay," I said. "I'll do it." Even though I had to do this in front of my peers, facing the wrath of God somehow seemed more palatable and less frightening than facing my mother's ire. A quick shake of the dice told me God would be more forgiving.

At church service that afternoon, I slunk up to the altar, knelt, and was saved. I asked Jesus to come into my heart. I said how sorry I was for all the things I had done. In retrospect, I think what I regretted most was that I had been caught.

Everyone cheered and clapped for me. We sang "What a Friend We Have in Jesus" and "For God So Loved the World." Then we made big posters out of colored construction paper that boldly announced "JESUS IS IN YOUR HEART."

We were all so happy that afternoon. The counselors rejoiced for the lost soul they had led to salvation. The other children were delighted (probably because it was me and not them who had been caught). And I was happy, too.

Mother wasn't called.

We did a repeat performance, including another trip to the altar, along with the singing, the cheering, and the poster making, the following day. The counselors wanted to make sure the experience "took." I left camp that year feeling good. But it didn't have the impact everyone hoped for. The moment I returned home, I headed straightaway for the cupboard under the kitchen sink and that bottle of Jack Daniels.

Ten years would pass before I would find my way into chemical dependency treatment and the twelve-step program that ultimately saved my life. And thirty-five years would elapse from the time I made the poster proclaiming Jesus Was in My Heart before I would understand what those colorful words I cut and pasted that day really meant.

For most of the years of my life, I thought they meant I had to jam a porcelain statue of Jesus into my heart. Although I considered myself a Christian, that vision didn't work for me. It didn't make sense.

Then, on my trip through the western United States in 1995, I wandered into the Sanctuario de Chimayo. The Sanctuario is a New Mexican church rich in folklore about the healing powers of the ground beneath its foundation. This dirt, this earth, is said to be sacred and holy, containing powers similar to that of the water in Lourdes. Crutches line the walls in the back room of the church, physical evidence of the healing miracles that have supposedly occurred here. Daily, for almost two weeks, I watched people walk, limp, and sometimes be carried into this church.

In the Sanctuario where so many flocked for a miracle, I too saw a flash of light. I finally understood what it meant to have Jesus in your heart. Whether they had known it or not, those well-intentioned, hand-wringing, soul-saving camp counselors from northern Minnesota were talking about the value and importance of each of our hearts. Hallelujah! I didn't have to keep trying to jam that porcelain statue into my chest anymore.

"It takes a lot to get out of bed each day and live life with passion and an open heart," Nichole said one day shortly before I left on this trip to the Middle East.

"Yes, it does," I agreed. "It certainly does."

They were all talking about the same thing—the camp counselors, my daughter, and now in the Nile River Papyrus shop, this intricate Egyptian picture hanging on the wall.

An open heart is as light as or lighter than a feather. And Jesus is in that heart.

"I'll take that one," I said, pointing to the picture about paradise.

I continued to look around the store. It took me only moments to spot it. It looked almost like a Celtic cross. It was gold. The top was rounded. A crossbar ran through the middle. On closer inspection, I saw that it was a key.

"What's that?" I asked.

"It's an ancient Egyptian symbol," the shop-keeper said. "The ankh. It's the key to power in this world."

The merchant took the simple painting off the wall, and I held it in my hand.

I was right. There was a key to power and life. I had suspected it all along. The Egyptians had known it for five thousand years. Maybe that was the reason for the camels' mysterious smiles. But my friend had been right, too. It wasn't really a secret and it wasn't out of reach.

The key to power wasn't in all the things I had done, the people I had talked to, the crystals on my desk, or the books on my shelves.

I had held it in my hand all the time. It's where all the hard work and all my endeavors had led.

The key to life and power is simple. It's knowing who we are. It's knowing what we think, what we feel, what we believe, what we know, and even what we sense. It's understanding where we've been, where we are, and where we want to go. That's often different from who we think we should be, from whom others want us to be, tell us to be, and sometimes even tell us we are.

There are many drugs that can injure the body and deaden the soul—cocaine, alcohol, heroin, marijuana. But there are other drugs whose narcotic power we overlook. Disillusionment and betrayal can grind away at our souls until all our faith and hope are gone. The cumulative effect of a lifetime of disappointments can leave us wandering around confused, lost, and dulled. Whether it happens in one moment or over many years, losing faith deadens the spirit like a syringe filled with heroin or a line of coke. The most debilitating drug on this planet besides losing faith in God is when we stop believing in ourselves.

I'll take it," I said. "I've been looking for that for a long time."

Shortly after I paid for my pictures, half price, Essam returned to the store. We had a quiet afternoon, sitting in the sandlot, watching an Egyptian version of *Candid Camera*, the famous old television show. Then I went to my hotel. I wanted to get a good night's rest. Tomorrow I was going into the pyramids of Giza.

Today, I had found the key to power in this life and in this world. Now I was ready to get my "special powers."

I STOPPED TALKING AND GLARED at the deceptively innocent looking female torturing me at the airport in Tel Aviv.

She wasn't intimidated.

"Show me the rest of your notes," she said.

I pulled out another sheet of paper. "I've got this," I said. "But it's not going to mean anything to you."

"Read it to me," the interrogator said.

"It's from a conversation with my nineteen-year-old daughter. It's just an idea—a concept—for this book."

"Tell me what it says," the interrogator said.

I looked at the words written on the piece of paper I held in my hand. I felt so embarrassed. Explaining this was going to be the toughest one of all.

chapter 10

Pyramid Power

From the Hanging Gardens of Babylon to the Pharos Lighthouse of Alexandria, the pyramids of Egypt are the only one of the Seven Wonders of the Ancient World that still remain intact. After thousands of years, these massive man-made structures also still remain shrouded in mystery.

From composite pictures drawn by archaeologists, scholars, and historians, we now understand that these colossal constructions were monuments to death—temples built of stone and filled with treasures to provide a luxurious dwelling place for nobility who had entered the realm of existence called the afterlife.

The dead could not necessarily take their riches with them into this mystical next world, but ancient Egyptians of nobility believed that they could come back and enjoy the treasures they had accumulated in this world if their possessions were carefully placed inside the tomb. They also believed at first that entrance into the afterlife was granted only to those of nobility. And this afterlife could be achieved only if the body were preserved so the soul could return to it. The culture developed a sophisticated and successful method of preserving bodies called mummification. Positioning of the body was important, too. The mummified bodies were placed under the exact center of the pyramid. And the pyramids were constructed on the west side of the Nile River because the Egyptians believed that the dwelling place of the deceased was in the direction of the setting sun.

It is said that people love a great mystery. That term—"great mystery"—aptly describes the Great Pyramids of Giza. Although they are a wonder of the ancient world, they *are* the physical embodiment of the word "mystery" in contemporary culture.

How this ancient civilization constructed these mammoth structures has caused much speculation and remains an enigma. Over two million stone blocks, each weighing about two and a half tons, were transported and carefully positioned to build King Khufu's pyramid alone—the largest of the three pyramids of Giza. Were the pyramids the result of much grunting, groaning, and primitive manual labor? Or were they constructed, as some people speculate, using innovative methods and tools that have since disappeared but, if rediscovered, would rival space-age technology?

When these pyramids were constructed now puzzles some historians and archaeologists. While many experts have surmised and long agreed that the pyramids of Giza date back to about forty-three hundred years ago, other scholars such as Joseph Jochmans are now stirring the historical and archaeological pot by suggesting that these mysterious monuments may have been built as long as twelve thousand years ago.

Although many puzzling aspects surround the "how," "when," and even the "why" of these pyramids, the ultimate mystery of these colossal tombs is the aspect perhaps least discussed by historians and most cloaked in legend. It is the secret surrounding the supernatural powers the pyramids are said to possess. The Great Pyramids of Giza may have been a gateway to the afterworld at the time they were constructed to entomb pharaohs Khufu, Khafre, and Menkure. But many of the millions of tourists who flock annually to Giza—despite threats of terrorism and war—and many local inhabitants, like Essam, believe that these pyramids are now, more than ever, a cabalistic portal—a gateway where passers-by can touch the edges of a world unknown.

My guide for this long-awaited expedition to get these special powers was again Essam's seventeen-year-old nephew. He explained the mystery of the pyramids differently while we were horseback riding to get there. It was mid-afternoon. We had just scaled the side of a rocky hill. Now we were passing through a desert graveyard, the local burial ground for those not of noble birth.

"It's better to be buried in a pyramid," the young guide said, pointing to the dusty graves. "Otherwise the wind blows the sand away and robbers steal all the treasures."

Essam had been talking to me about going into the pyramids to meditate since the night we first met.

I didn't understand what he meant about "getting the powers." Nor did I especially *believe* him. But I had followed his strict instructions anyway. I had my four small white candles in my backpack. I was dressed in white. And to my great embarrassment, I was wearing a white cotton cloth on my head, held in place by a woven green band.

I had argued with Essam about wearing this kerchief on my head, but he had insisted. "If you want to get the special powers, you must wear that white cloth," he said.

Grumbling all the while, I had purchased the white head covering from one of the young merchants hawking his wares on the path that led from the perfume store to the pyramids. It cost two dollars and fifty cents.

Riding the horse across the desert, headed for one of the smaller step pyramids, I felt more like a cheap tourist imitation of an Arab sheik than I did an enlightened woman on her way to becoming empowered.

I knew there was something special about the pyramids. I felt it my first night in Cairo, when I had been drawn to them. I felt it even when that menacing group of men made a run at me by the fence. I felt the powers of the pyramids each time I came close to them during my stay here. Their influence on the village of Giza was undeniable.

But I had never particularly fantasized about going into a burial tomb to meditate—even one of these colossal stone monuments. I didn't understand what mysterious powers could possibly be inside the pyramids or how these powers could possibly affect me. Although I liked, respected, and trusted Essam, I secretly thought this whole ordeal of going into the pyramids and "getting the powers" was a tourist gimmick.

If there's so much power here, why are so many people living in poverty? Why are the women so trapped? And why do these people drive the way they do?

I was skeptical. I was skeptical about the "special pyramid powers." I was skeptical about crawling around inside a tomb. And I was skeptical about wearing this stupid white rag on my head.

After clearing the mountainside and the graveyard, I loosened my hold on the reins, nudged the horse with my heels, and began galloping across the stretch of desert that separated me from the pyramids. I was still baffled by how quickly I had taken to horseback riding. But I didn't question that mystery. It was as if I had been riding horses all my life.

The ability to break through a barrier or block in one moment and begin doing something that in the past appeared unfathomable was awe-inspiring, yet I almost took it for granted. *If people could do that, I thought, they could do almost anything. It's about our perception, our fears, and the limitations we place on ourselves.*

When we neared the Great Pyramids, my guide pointed to one of the smaller pyramids that stood at the edge of the three large ones. The smaller pyramids were the burial tombs for the queens and relatives of the pharaohs, he said. We were headed there.

We rode to a small hut that housed the pyramid guard. My guide took my horse's reins and tied up both horses. Soon, a frowning bulk of sun-dried man emerged from the hut and approached me. He was wearing a uniform. He was the official pyramid guard. He would take me inside to meditate and get my powers.

Essam had prepared me for this. I knew I would have to pay off the guard for allowing me private entrance into the pyramid. Well, not really pay him off—I was to tip him. But Essam had instructed me not to pay the guard until after I finished meditating.

The guard led us on foot to the pyramid entrance—a small hole in the side of the pyramid. The guard asked if I was ready. I said yes and showed him my four white candles. The guard shook his head no. *He* had four white candles he wanted me to use. He said he wanted to be sure I got the powers.

And probably wants to be sure he gets a bigger tip, I thought.

"Okay," I said. "We'll use your candles."

The bulky guard squeezed himself through the small opening in the side of the pyramid. I followed him, trying to climb in head first. That didn't work. So I hoisted myself up and lowered myself in, feet first. In an instant, I went from blazing desert sunlight to the pitch-black interior of this tomb. We walked hunched over through a narrow passageway that was only about three feet high. My guide followed behind me. After a few moments, the guard in front of me stopped and lit one of the candles.

I looked around the musty, dank interior. The walls flickered with gentle light from the candle. The rock was crumbling. It was the palest shade of yellow, almost off-white in color.

We followed a circular trail leading to the heart of the tomb. After a while, we were able to stand almost straight. Then we came to a juncture. One passage led to the right, one veered to the left. We went left. After walking a short distance, we reached a dead end, a small womblike room in the center of the pyramid. The ground was littered with crumbling rock. A natural ledge about three feet off the ground encircled the area of this three-sided cubbyhole.

The guard dripped a few drops of candle wax onto the ledge from the candle he held in his hand, then stuck the candle firmly in place. Then he lit the remaining three candles, carefully positioning them equidistant apart on the ledge, creating a semicircle of light. I sat down on the ground, with my back to the dead-end wall of the small room, and adjusted the white kerchief on my head.

The pyramid guard and my guide wished me luck in getting the powers. Then they left me alone.

I sat on the floor of the tomb. This is ludicrous, I thought. What am I doing? Is this really how one finds enlightenment? It seemed more like the height of absurdity to me.

I didn't know what to do next.

This wasn't the first time my quest for enlightenment had left me feeling in the dark.

A year ago, on my journey through the western United States, I had wandered into a Native American sweat lodge in Sedona, Arizona. I understood that it was a sacred ritual symbolizing spiritual cleansing and purification. But that was all I understood. I dutifully and respectfully stood and allowed myself to be purified with sage smoke before I entered the tent. Then I climbed through the flap with the other participants. I watched as the fire keeper brought glowing hot rocks into the tent, placing them in an indentation in the ground. I could see that the rocks would create the heat that would make us sweat. But I wished I had an instruction manual.

I listened attentively, sweating, huddled in the tent, as the old Native American shaman began the ceremony with a prayer. My anxiety heightened as it became apparent that participants were expected to say something aloud. I wanted to fit into the rhythm of the experience. I wanted to get all I could out of it. I wanted to do it right.

Sweat dripped down my face. I leaned forward intently, hanging on every word the shaman uttered.

"And now we will honor the spirit of yeast," she said, "who brings us . . ."

I lurched back. The spirit of yeast? I thought. What does that mean? My mind raced. I tried to figure out if we were honoring bread, or agriculture, and what I could say about that when it became my turn. I was thinking so hard I could barely listen. All the while, I struggled to act calm and enlightened.

I mumbled something when it became my time to speak.

"And now we will thank the spirit of the West," the shaman said next.

Oh, I thought. The Spirit of the East. Now I get it.

On another occasion, I had gone to my doctor, a holistic healing professional, for almost two years before I understood what he was talking about. During that time, he had regularly referred to my "orc" field. I had no idea what he was saying. None whatsoever. I knew vaguely that he was talking about the energy that was part of me and that surrounded my physical body. The work with this healing professional had been profound. It had helped me greatly. So I didn't question him about my "orc" field. I assumed it was some new discovery everyone but me knew. After almost two years, while I was reading a book, I finally understood. My doctor, my healer, had been talking about my "auric" field.

There were a lot of things about life that I just didn't get. Sitting in this tomb on the edge of the

Sahara Desert, I didn't understand what I was supposed to do now. But, if sitting here with a kerchief on my head was going to help me get one inch closer to the missing piece, then I would try it. I really wanted to be enlightened. I really wanted "the powers"—if there were any special powers to be had.

I will do what I know to—meditate, I thought.

I looked around the area where I sat. I picked up a couple pieces of the light crumbling rock and held one stone in each hand.

I would begin by praying.

First, I said the Lord's Prayer. "Our Father, who art in Heaven, hallowed be thy name. Thy Kingdom come, thy will be done, on earth as it is in heaven. Give us this day our daily bread, and forgive us our trespasses as we forgive those who trespass against us. And lead us not into temptation, but deliver us from evil. For thine is the kingdom, and the power, and the glory, forever and ever."

Next, I said the Ave Maria. "Hail Mary, full of grace, the Lord is with you. Blessed are you among women, and blessed is the fruit of your womb, Jesus. Holy Mary, Mother of God, pray for us sinners now and at the hour of our death. Amen."

Then, I did a Buddhist chant I had learned. *"Om ah hung vara guru padme siddi hung. Om mani pami hung."*

There, I thought. I sat for a moment. I was a lot dustier. The candles had melted some. Other than that, nothing had changed. I felt exactly the same as I had before I entered this mystical pyramid.

I closed my eyes and tried to concentrate, but the droning voices of two people talking outside the cubbyhole distracted me. I wondered how much these people had paid for this enlightening experience.

"Shhhhh," I said loudly. "I'm *meditating*."

Next, I tried some less formal prayers. I prayed for the people I loved—my daughter, my son, my family and friends. I prayed for the people I resented. I finished with some prayers of gratitude, counting and expounding on my blessings.

Then I opened my eyes and looked around. Nothing was happening yet.

I reclined on the ground, using my backpack for a pillow. Now I would "breathe my *chakras*," an exercise my holistic doctor had recently taught me. *Chakras* are thought to be the energy centers, or openings in the body. Deliberately envisioning them and breathing into them during meditation supposedly clears out residue and opens us to power.

I visualized breathing a spinning circle of color for each *chakra*, starting at the bottom, or root *chakra*, and working my way up to the crown. I started with red at the bottom, at the base of my spine. Then I envisioned an orange circle slightly below my belly button. Next, I saw a spinning yellow circle in my solar plexus, then green for the heart, blue in the throat, purple on my forehead, and white at the crown. I went up the body, then down the body, imagining the colorful circles rapidly spinning counterclockwise. I did this for ten or fifteen minutes with my eyes closed, breathing deeply.

I thought I started to see "The Light," but when I opened my eyes, I saw it was just the flickering from the candle flames.

I still felt exactly the same as I had before entering this tomb.

Now I was out of things to do. I sat there, looking around, feeling stupid, watching the candles burn. I wished the two men would come back for me. I wished I wasn't wearing this ridiculous hankie on my head. I wished I had a *shisha* with some tobacco in it now.

I felt as if I had failed.

I sat, and sat, and sat, waiting . . . for at least an hour. Nothing happened. Nothing was going to happen. I wanted to leave. "Help," I began to yell softly. "Please come and get me."

The guides appeared instantly at the entrance to the cubbyhole. "What took you so long?" I said.

"We were just sitting around the corner," the guide said. "That was us talking. *We* were waiting for *you*."

I grabbed my backpack and followed the two men out the narrow passageway, through the hole in the side of the pyramid, out into the bright light of the Sahara Desert. I tried to give the pyramid guard the amount of money Essam had recommended, but the guard made such a scowling face that I immediately gave him some more. Then my guide and I rode the horses back to the sandlot.

I dismounted, tipped the young man who had escorted me on my journey into enlightenment, and went to find Essam to say good-bye.

I was thirsty, dirty, dusty, and disheartened. I was also done for the day.

"Did you get the powers?" Essam asked earnestly.

"Yes," I lied, "I did."

What a crock, I thought, in the cab on the way back to my hotel. I have really and truly outdone myself this time.

When I returned to my hotel room, I flopped down on the bed and stared at the ceiling.

I felt cheapened, stupid, and betrayed—again.

I don't know when it happened, but at some point I stopped thinking and began talking out loud.

"I don't get it," I said. "I absolutely and totally don't get it. I am so sick of chasing the truth. I'm so sick of the pain on this basically uninhabitable planet. I'm sick of trying to make a life and failing. I'm sick of getting back up again each time, trying again, just to stumble and fail again. I'm sick of going through pain, then calling it a learning experience, only to have neither the pain nor the learning ever end. I'm sick of trying harder, doing better, and being someone I'm not. The whole thing is a crock.

"What's the point?" I screamed at the ceiling. "Why do we have to come here if all of life is going to conspire against us to make it as hard as it can possibly be?"

Life *hurt*. I hurt. My spirit hurt. My emotions hurt. And my butt hurt from horseback riding.

I felt as though I'd been fighting the devil every step of the way.

"Oh, I can keep doing this," I said aloud. "I can keep going through each disappointing experience. I can keep struggling. I always survive, don't I? I've done it for almost forty-eight years. I'm a strong woman. I go through whatever it is I need to go through. And I do it like a trooper. Yup, that's me. I'm so good at dealing with pain, disappointment, heartache, betrayal, and problems. I've learned how to be grateful for every bit of it. I've learned how to breathe into the pain. I've learned how to get through, get around, make the best of, transform, and even turn it into healing for other people. Yeah, I can do it. I've turned it into an art . . .

That's what this is about, I thought suddenly. I got up off the bed and stood in the middle of my hotel room. "Eureka!" I said. "I've got it!"

I flashed back to the summer before this trip.

One day Nichole stopped by the house. She was going through a hard summer—that transition from being a child to an adult. She had been groveling around in emotional muck for months. That day, she was complaining about her pain—about all the pain in life.

"You ought to be happy," I said. "Today's Friday."

She just stared at me. "Does your pain end on Fridays?" she said.

We listened to Janis Joplin belt out "Me and Bobby McGee" and "Get It While You Can" on the stereo, then Nichole told me the story of how she thought life really worked.

"My girlfriend Jen and I figured it out over lunch," she explained. "There's two kinds of people in this world: the pigs and the vampires. The pigs think they're going to be happy when they buy a new home,

get married, get a new car, or get a new job. They really believe those little things will stop the pain. And for them it does, kind of. They just go bowling, or they golf, and that's enough. The vampires are different. They've been through some kind of tunnel, some kind of experience that's really changed them. And it's not that they've never come out. They just get changed by it. They know too much. They do all the same things pigs do. They get new cars, they move, they get married, they take new jobs. But they know that these things are never going to make them happy. They know that life is going to hurt sometimes, at least a little bit. And sometimes, it's gonna hurt a lot."

It took me a while to realize Nichole wasn't using the word "vampires" the way I usually thought of that word. She wasn't talking about werewolves, monsters, bloodsuckers, or human parasites. She was talking about pigs and vampires the way a college girl would talk about two football teams. They were just terms, or names, for people on the teams of life.

"It's not that vampires are never happy," Nichole said. "But they're happy in a different way. They feel all their feelings. And sometimes they have moments of pure joy. But they know those moments aren't forever. They move right on to the next feeling and experience.

"In some ways," Nichole said, "the vampires are even happier than the pigs because vampires know how they really feel. They tell the truth and people like that. People like being around them, even though, for the most part, vampires' lives suck. But they take the pain and they turn it into something more. They do something with it."

I flashed back to a letter I had received from a young man I met on Christmas Day, the day I first saw the crescent moon and star in the sky.

He was in his early twenties. He and his mother were friends of a friend of mine. They had joined Nichole and me and our mutual friend for Christmas dinner. In the year past, this young man had almost died. Then he had made a decision to come back to life, a decision that made him and his mother happy.

"My dream is also to be a storyteller," he wrote to me in a letter thanking me for the day. "I sometimes wonder if that's why I survived—to give back something of what I've learned. I hope that one of my purposes on this planet is to use the perspective gained from tragedy to illuminate life. I think it is in reaching out to the universe and deeply within ourselves that allows us to transcend these experiences. It is what allows us to turn tragedy into a life force for

ourselves and others. It is what allows us to transcend surviving."

I flashed back to the beginning of this trip in Paris, when I had whisked through the Museum of Man and the Louvre. That's what that was all about, I thought. It was the setup, the kickoff, for this adventure. It led directly to today. It was all right there. I had seen the eternal themes of life on this planet—birth, family, health, marriage, religion, divination, and death—and the art that results from all the anguish and joy of those experiences—the rich and treasured art that fills the halls of the Louvre.

Evolution wasn't something that may or may not have happened once, at the beginning of time. Our planet, the life and people on it, continually evolve. As we grind through each issue and theme, the work and art we create embody these experiences for the rest of the world. Our creations help us evolve, but our lives and our work help others evolve, too.

We're not just here to live our lives and to create our art. We're part of the art being created.

For a long, long time—somewhere in the back of my mind—lurked the codependent exhortation that if I really loved God and truly wanted to serve on this planet, I would force myself to take vows of chastity and poverty and live the lives of the people I served.

Now, in the hotel room in Cairo, I began to see that's exactly what many of us had been doing all along. We were having the range of human experiences and emotions of the people we would later serve.

Lives without pain, comedy, drama, irony, romance, suffering, some foolishness, and a dash of unrequited love would be like going to see a movie without a plot. It's not that life is *only* pain, suffering, drama, and tragedy, but those elements are part of it. And always have been.

From the raw material of these experiences came the art we would create—the art of living our lives and the art we create in our work. So often the experiences I wanted to deny were the raw material that had been handed to me to shape and form into truth and into art. Nichole had been correct. This way of living and creating art involves speaking the truth. My new friend, the one who had written me a letter, had been correct too. This way of living, working, and approaching our lives allows us to transcend survival and martyrdom, and it illuminates the truth for others. It's not the art of living happily ever after. It's the art of learning to live joyfully.

It is the walk of the Christ.

I have a friend, a diva, an opera singer from the East Coast. Early on in her career, when she was a

beautiful young woman, she resonated to the Mozart
Requiem. *Her instructor at the Juilliard School of*
Music, Leonard Bernstein, asked her then why such a
young woman with a brilliant future was so interested
in such a heavy work. She replied that she didn't know,
she just was. Over the years, she continued to sing.
Then she married and gave birth to two beautiful sons.
When her youngest son was twenty, he was killed in a
motorcycle crash.

"Now I know why I was so passionate about the
Requiem," *she said. "It was my destiny to sing that song*
from the depths of my soul. The problem was," my diva
friend said, "by the time I learned to sing the Requiem
with passion and understanding, I was so embittered
and broken-hearted I no longer wanted to sing."

My diva friend told me another story about a com-
poser who lived in another time. This composer con-
sidered himself a craftsman, someone who diligently
worked at the job of composing music each day the
way a shopkeeper goes to his store or a dressmaker fits
and sews dresses.

The craftsman-composer had hit a wall with his
creativity and his work. He was stuck. He couldn't
write a note. One day, while feeling tormented over his
dilemma of not being able to write music, the composer
opened his window. Outside, he heard three notes

being played beautifully on a horn. The notes seemed to be coming from a barn nearby. Each day for days, when he opened the window, the composer heard these same three beautiful notes being played. Finally, the composer left his room and went in search of the origin of these three hauntingly beautiful sounds. He then discovered a young boy hiding in the barn playing a horn.

The composer talked to the boy for a while. He learned that the boy's father beat the boy terribly and refused to let the boy play music. To avoid the daily beatings and have the freedom to play his horn, the boy hid in the barn and played the only three notes he knew.

The craftsman-composer went on to use these three beautiful notes as the inspiration and foundation for the next piece of music he would write—the lovely, lilting "Strauss Waltz" by Johann Strauss.

Some of us hear and learn to sing a wide range of emotional notes in our lives. Others learn to sing or play only a few. It doesn't matter how many notes we're called to sing. What matters is that we sing them the best, the purest, the finest we are able. When we do, our lives and work not only bring healing to the world, our work brings healing to ourselves.

In an afterword to the stories she told me, my diva friend told me something else. If we struggle and work to learn our craft of living and creating with emotional honesty and joy, we will train our voices and our souls to sing the final, high, resonating sound that is the purest note in the scale, the one divas work so hard to achieve.

It is the full, rich tone of peace.

In less than half an hour, in my hotel room in downtown Cairo, a lifetime of dissatisfaction had shown its grim face for what it was. It was as though a vortex had whirled through me, cleansing me of these dark remnants from my past.

These grim emotional secrets that had been buried in me were not necessarily news. I had lived with, through, and in spite of them for years. What was an innovative thought was that I could be healed, or freed, from these beliefs and emotions that had colored my vision and spirit for so long.

I wasn't elated or euphoric. But my emotional state had spun around distinctly for the better. In the whirlwind that followed my excursion into the pyramid, my skepticism had dissipated. So had my contempt. In its place, I now felt excitement, a rush of joy, and a sense of purpose that had been missing for a long time.

Something *had* happened inside that mysterious tomb. There was a power there. I could feel and see it now. This journey, this grueling excursion, was leading someplace. It had a *point*. Even though it hadn't *felt* as if anything was happening, something important and magnificent had been taking place all along.

Mysteries, secrets, ancient wisdom, and special powers had been buried in these tombs. Now this wisdom and these powers were being released. I had touched the edges of a world unknown.

The mystery of my life was being revealed.

UNTIL NOW, I HAD BEEN LIVING out of an unpacked suitcase in one room in a downtown Cairo hotel. I had been indecisive about how long I would stay in Cairo and exactly where I would go next. I had originally planned to finish my trip by flying to Greece and writing my book there—but that leg of the trip still hadn't materialized.

Despite the language barriers, the unbearably chaotic traffic, the overcrowding, my great caution about the food, my lingering stomachache, and the large number of people who wanted gratuities whether or not they had performed a service, Cairo—and its suburb, Giza—had become my home.

I immediately decided what to do next. There are times and places of heightened and accelerated spiritual growth. I had just entered one.

I would stay in Egypt and write my book.

WHAT IS WRITTEN ON THAT piece of paper you're hiding from me?" demanded the interrogator in Tel Aviv.

I sheepishly showed her the two words scrawled at the bottom of the sheet. "Vampire Art," I said. "That's all it says. It's a note to myself."

"I see," my interrogator said.

"Open your computer," she said. "I want to see what you've written in there."

"I would gladly show you what's in my computer," I said. "But there's nothing in there to show. I didn't get around to writing. Something happened that changed my plans."

She looked at me as if she didn't believe what I had just said.

I began to stumble through the next part of my story. I didn't completely understand the shift yet either—the one that had wrested me out of Egypt and propelled me into the interrogation first in Cairo and now here in Tel Aviv.

What I couldn't yet explain was about to become clear.

chapter 11

The Pounding
Continues

Essam had given me the address of a small hotel in a residential neighborhood close to Giza. He had been gently harping at me for days about moving to a less expensive hotel, one where I could feel more settled and at home. Now I decided to explore and make that move.

When I went to check out the hotel, the manager showed me a suite. It was nothing fancy—basic Egyptian decor. But the price was right. It was almost like an apartment. It had a large bathroom, a living room, *and* a bedroom. It would be a perfect place to write. I'd be only a few minutes from the desert. I could unpack my computer, set up shop, and alternate times of intense work with powerful meditation sessions in the pyramids.

The ancient energy I had tapped into here would keep me highly charged.

I returned to the hotel in downtown Cairo, checked out, and loaded my belongings in a taxi. Instead of going directly to the hotel, I headed for the sandlot. I wanted to return to the pyramids for another dose of their powers.

I left my belongings at the perfume shop and mounted a camel for my trek to the small, potent pyramid that had unleashed its energy on me yesterday. I had packed away my white head covering in my suitcase. I didn't think wearing it today would be necessary. But Essam insisted that I again wear white "to get the powers."

As the camel clopped down the narrow path on the way to the desert, I purchased yet another white cloth and stuck it on my head. I didn't understand what had taken place in the pyramid. I didn't see how wearing a white rag on my head connected to this mystery. But undeniably, yesterday *had* affected me greatly. I wanted more—even if meant looking ridiculous.

Essam's young nephew rode alongside me again. I smiled at the same bulky sun-withered pyramid guard and followed him through the tiny opening in the side of the tomb. I crouched down and walked through the narrow curving passageway. The guard placed four white candles on the rim encircling the small room in the center of the pyramid. He and my guide then departed, leaving me alone to receive more of the "special powers."

This time, I sat cross-legged on the floor, closed my eyes, and asked God to help me. I began to meditate, breathing in the air and energy of this dank mysterious vortex. In moments, just seconds, it hit me. It entered through my crown.

The force of the energy whipped me backwards, knocking me flat on the ground. The hair on my arms stood up, electrified. From my head to my toes, this mysterious vortex whirled through me with the force of a tornado, charging me with its powers.

It had probably done the same thing yesterday, but I'd been too clogged with my own dank beliefs and dark emotional residues to feel it. Today, I could feel it while it was happening.

Yesterday had been a critical step—a preparation for today.

There are higher places we can go to connect with ancient energies, power, and wisdom that have been entombed and hidden from sight. The purpose of the powerful energy being unleashed is to clear us out so these long-forgotten powers can manifest in each of us.

When I finished meditating, I tipped the guard, rode the camel back to the sandlot, paid my guide, and thanked Essam. I made tentative plans to return to Essam and the pyramids in a few days. I was ready to get to work.

When I arrived at my new home, the small hotel near Giza, the owner checked me in and gave me a key to my room. I took the slow, creaking elevator to the ninth floor, went to the room number I had been assigned, and opened the door.

I looked around, my eyes widening in disbelief. This room was dark, and it was the size of a large closet—nothing like the apartment I had been shown before. I walked to the one small window, opened the grimy curtains, and looked outside. The room was not only small and dark, it directly over-looked a construction site.

This triggered a memory, an unpleasant one that had begun the summer before this trip.

I was renting a small cottage by the sea. I could hear the waves from every room in my little house. The warm California sun rarely hid behind the clouds. I could write, walk on the beach, go for a swim in the ocean after my morning coffee. I could live and write my books with nature at my side. It wasn't necessarily a dream home, but it was heaven to me—until the pounding began.

It started with a simple "for sale" sign that went up on the house next door. Soon new owners purchased the property—a sprawling mansion that dwarfed my little cottage. The new owners gutted their huge house and began major reconstruction. In California, there is often little space between the homes. Their home was only a few feet from my office, my bedroom, and my living room. Every morning, the noise from the hammering, the radios, and the loud voices of the laborers woke me before my alarm, which was set for 7:00 A.M. Most days, the noise sounded as if it came from my living room.

The pounding continued day after day after day— six and sometimes seven days a week.

It would go on for almost a year.

The noise seemed to intensify each time I went in my office to work. Even the healing forces of nature—the sun, fresh air, and frothy surf—weren't enough to diminish the colossally annoying forces of the workers' hammering blows.

I explored moving. I looked at over fifty other dwellings. No door opened for me there. I was stuck living next to a construction site. I tried to live with the situation as best I could, acknowledging my neighbors' right to renovate and my right to be annoyed. But the combination of their noise and my frustration blocked me from working or living in peace.

Now in Giza, as I looked out from this tiny, dark room and saw the sprawling construction site loaded with jackhammers, mesh fencing, and loud-talking workers, I just shook my head. This isn't going to work, I thought. It's not going to work at all.

I returned to the lobby and complained to the manager.

"This is not the room you showed me originally," I said. "I want a large room like the one I saw before. I want windows, so light can get in. And I don't want to live and sleep next to a construction site. I'm planning on working here. I told you that before. I need peace and quiet."

The manager, an older, polished Arabian gentleman dressed in a suit, suddenly developed a problem speaking English. He acted as if he didn't understand, stumbled over words, balked a bit, then finally agreed to give me a better room—the only other room he said was available. Naturally, he would have to raise the price. I said that was fine but asked to see the room first. He showed me the room. It was the same one he had originally shown me.

I grilled him then.

"Will it be quiet here?" I asked.

"Yes," he said.

"Do you promise?" I asked.

"Yes," he said, assuring me the room would be everything I wanted. I transferred my luggage and, for the first time since leaving the United States, unpacked. I hung my clothes in the closet. I put my smaller garments in the drawers. I unpacked my bath products, my hair products, and my mementos. I spent the entire evening setting up my room. I was halfway around the world from where I lived, but I wanted to make myself feel comfortable.

The following day, I finally unpacked my computer too. I hooked up the electrical adapter I had brought to accommodate the foreign voltage. Then I turned on the computer, opened a fresh new file, and typed one or two words, trying to get my lead. That's when it began.

It started with one loud pound. Seconds later, another loud pound followed. Then, another.

Soon the pounds turned into continuous, irregularly paced slams that shook the walls, the floor, and the legs of the little table where I sat, staring into my fresh new file.

I didn't know who was making this noise but my irritation increased with each wall-shaking slam. I told myself to ignore the pounding. Then my stomach started to hurt. It ached. I forced myself to focus on the blank computer screen and tried to think up words to write. The harder I tried to focus, the harder the pounding shook the walls and my concentration, and the more my stomach hurt.

What's wrong with me that I can't handle a little pounding? I thought. Just buck up, do your work, and ignore the noise.

I couldn't ignore it.

Finally, I pushed my chair away from the table and walked to the outside corridor. I looked around, trying to locate the source of the noise and my aggravation. I didn't have to go far. The door to the room next to mine was wide open. A dark, rail-thin man sat cross-legged on the floor, a few inches from the wall. In his hand, he held a large mallet—the biggest hammer I had ever seen. Every few seconds, he raised the mallet over his head and took a whack at the wall. Each blow cracked off a tiny piece of the thick, concrete-like plaster that comprised these old Egyptian walls.

The man wasn't wielding the hammer fast, but he was smacking hard. It looked as if he was yet to find his rhythm. The entire hole he had made in the wall measured less than a square foot.

"Excuse me," I said.

He looked my way.

"How long is this pounding going to continue?" I asked.

He looked around the room and gestured. "Until all the walls are down," he said.

I took a deep breath, thanked him, and returned to my room.

I tried going back to my writing and ignoring the noise. That didn't work. The more I tried to ignore the pounding, the louder it sounded. Each time I heard the thud of the hammer hitting the wall, I began anticipating the next blow.

I pushed away from the desk and decided to meditate. I lay down on the bed, closed my eyes, relaxed my body, and allowed myself to sink into a deep, almost

hypnotic state—imaging white light around me, trying to recreate the power I had felt surge through me
in the pyramid. As I relaxed more and more, I deliberately programmed a thought into my mind: when I
come out of this state, I will know what to do next.
I will go deep within myself. The answer I need will
be there.

I meditated for almost an hour.

When I arose, I felt calm and serene. The pounding continued, but my anxiety had diminished. In
just a few moments, the answer came to me, seem-
ingly from nowhere. The solution surprised me but
expressed itself with crystal clarity.

I knew what I had to do.

It was time to leave. It was time to go home.

This trip—all parts of it—had been enlightening
and transformational. But I had found my story. I had
gotten what I needed. I was tired of pretending my
stomach didn't hurt. The pounding would continue—
I was obviously doomed to have it follow me around.
And I was beginning to gradually fade into this culture, which wasn't the purpose of this journey. For
many reasons—some that I understood and some
that I didn't see—it was clear that the same vortex
that had brought me here was now spitting me out.

I had been pushed to my limits. Enough was
enough.

A strange feeling settled in. I felt agitated, almost panicky. I didn't understand this feeling, but I knew what it meant. I wasn't being gently nudged out of Egypt. I was being pushed out as forcefully as I had been drawn here. It wasn't just time to leave. It was time to leave *now*. My Middle Eastern adventure had ended.

I went to the phone and called Wendy, back in the United States.

"See if you can get me out of here," I said. "See if there's a flight out tonight."

Wendy promised to call me back within the hour. I hung up the phone and started stuffing my clothes into suitcases. Shortly, the phone rang. I expected to hear Wendy's voice. It was Essam.

He asked how I was, and when I was coming to the sandlot again.

Essam had been so helpful in setting up a place for me to stay. He had so many events planned for the rest of this trip. I knew he was looking forward to my continued visit. I knew he would be disappointed by this sudden change in plans. I felt foolish after all he had done. I hoped he wouldn't feel as if I had let him down or betrayed him because I had changed my mind.

Once, while I was eating in a restaurant with Nichole and Will, the slice of pineapple Nichole was trying to cut had slipped off her fork, flown across the room, and landed at some other patron's foot. Nichole had covered her mouth with her hand and said, "Oops."

That's what I had to do now.

Essam sounded saddened at the news, but he was respectful of my decision to leave. I told him I was waiting for Wendy to call back with the flight information. If I could get out tonight I would swing by the perfume shop and say good-bye before I left. I hung up the phone and returned to packing. When I closed and locked my last suitcase, I realized Wendy still hadn't called.

By now, three hours had passed.

I felt agitated and confused. Wendy was reliable, dependable, and always on time. She did exactly what she said she would do. Although she was back in the United States, she had helped me navigate this entire trip.

I called her. She answered immediately.

"Where were you?" she said. "I've been trying to call you back. All the front desk would tell me is that you were gone for the day."

My agitation turned to mild paranoia.

Why would they tell her that? They knew I was here. I had called down and talked to the person at the front desk several times. I could see it all happening before my eyes. Nichole would have to fly over here, find me, and wrest me back home. She'd be doing a remake of *Not Without My Daughter,* a hair-raising real-life story about an American woman who refused to leave an Arab country until she could free her child. Only Nichole would be calling her book *Not Without My Mother.*

Wendy and I agreed on the phone that for whatever reason, something didn't feel quite right. And yes, it was time to go.

Then Wendy told me the good news. She could get me out on a flight tonight. I would have to fly from Cairo to Tel Aviv, and then sit in Tel Aviv for almost seven hours. From there, I'd pick up an Air France flight that would fly me directly to L.A.

I didn't think twice. If that was the door that was opening, I'd walk through it.

"Book me," I said. "If I hurry, I can make it."

I paid for my room, checked out of the hotel, hailed a taxi, and headed for Lotus Palace Perfumes. It was time for one last look at the sandlot. It was time to tell Essam good-bye.

I asked the cab driver to wait while I sat on the bench and talked for a while to Essam. This sudden parting was hard for both of us. We had become close friends. I thanked him for all his help, his warm hospitality, and all the lessons he had helped me to learn. We talked of things we might do in the future, if I were ever to return. Of course the women wanted to see me again, he said. The pyramids were waiting with more powers. And Essam could take me—and any friends or family I brought along—camping in the desert, riding camels by night and pitching and sleeping in Arabian tents during the hot desert days.

Essam excused himself for a moment, then returned bearing handfuls of gifts. He gave me bottles filled with colored desert sand, a metal commemorative plate, a figurine, and three stone replicas of the pyramids. I packed the gifts in my suitcase. Then, Essam placed in my hand three tiny blue stone beetles—scarabs—symbols of resurrection, rebirth, and eternal life.

I hugged him good-bye and said I would return someday, adding the words *"Insha'a Allah."*

I climbed into the cab, and we headed toward the airport. We had to drive through Giza and most of Cairo to get there. It was late. Time was running out. The already thick, unruly traffic would be steadily increasing until it reached its chaotic evening peak.

"Hurry," I told the driver, as we wound our way through the village of Giza.

He turned around to look at me. "Hurry?" he said, imitating me with an Arabic accent. Obviously, he didn't understand the word.

"Yes, hurry. Fast," I said, making a quick, sweeping gesture with my hand.

"Oh." He nodded in recognition. "Quickly!"

I turned around for one last look at the pyramids. Lit for the night shows, they glowed mystically on the desert skyline. I sank down into the seat and closed my eyes, preparing for the drive ahead. Now, my driver was dutifully *hurrying*.

A fleeting thought crossed my mind. *Don't relax too much. This trip isn't over yet.* I ignored it. I just wanted to go home.

I arrived at the Cairo airport half an hour before the plane was scheduled to depart. I checked my luggage through the first security check, then tried to get past the hoard of porters—some of whom didn't even touch my luggage—who held their hands out for a tip. One porter ran up to me and tried to grab the money hanging out of my pocket.

"Stop that. You're disgusting," I screamed under my breath. "You didn't even touch my luggage. Now get away."

I relaxed when I reached the next security check a few moments later. I thought I was home free. But it wasn't over yet. A young woman with dark hair suddenly approached me, then pulled me aside. That's when the interrogation began.

"I thought it was just a fluke that I had been held and interrogated in Cairo. When they finally released me, after I had broken down and cried, I didn't think about the incident again. I was simply glad it was over and happy to be on my way home. Now, after almost four hours of being grilled, held under the spotlight, and having my notes and computer examined here, I know it's more than a fluke," I said to the interrogator in Tel Aviv.

Something's going on here, I thought. Something more than meets the eye.

Seeing my frustration and anger, the chestnut-haired female grilling me suddenly switched gears. For the first time, she appeared sympathetic and almost human.

"I'm sorry this is taking so long," she said. "But we have many bomb threats in our country."

"I understand," I said. I hoped that meant she was going to stop.

It didn't. She immediately fired her next question my way.

"Do you have any more notes? Anything more you can show us?"

Why was I being tortured this way? What was going on? I didn't get it the first time, and I especially didn't get it now. I was standing here, dripping sweat, the *only* person detained in this airport.

I dug through my folder. "Here. This is it," I said. "This is all I can find. It's absolutely all I wrote."

"Read it to me," she said.

I started reading from the wrinkled piece of paper.

"It's not just about the things we do or don't do, although those things matter. It's not about always doing things the right way. And it's certainly not about doing things the way others tell us we should. It's about how we love and treat ourselves, how we respond to ourselves, how we talk to ourselves about the things we do—our life experiences, who we are, and where we've been. It's about giving ourselves that feeling of gentle, loving self-acceptance, the one we've wanted for so long.

"It's the spirit of a thing that counts overall," I read. "And this is a book about the spirit of self-love."

Suddenly, standing there reading to the interrogator from my wrinkled piece of paper, I got it. The lights came on in Tel Aviv. This interrogation wasn't punishment, nor was it torture—even though it certainly felt as if it was. The world wasn't against me. Life was trying to show and teach me something.

I was supposed to tell this interrogator my story. This wasn't an accident. *It was an important part of the book, the trip, and my life.*

I had been so busy feeling tormented I hadn't seen it. I didn't get it in Cairo, the first time it happened. But that was all right. Lessons don't go away. They keep repeating themselves until we do understand.

The second I saw this, the interrogation ceased.

The young woman smiled.

"You can go now," she said. "Have a good flight."

I reached the Air France gate minutes before the boarding call. As I walked down the ramp on the way to the plane, I realized something had slipped my mind. I had forgotten to show my interrogator the interview notes from my day trip to the terrorist hills in Algiers.

No sense stirring that pot, I thought. It was an honest mistake. Besides, I'll miss my flight.

Oops, again.

I settled into my seat on the plush French airliner. The country of France had shown me the beauty of its art in the Louvre and a history course in the eternal themes of life at the Museum of Man. Now the French were showing me something else, too. They knew how to enjoy the good things in life. I had even heard the French people were switching to a four-day work week. They were willing to take less pay to have more time to enjoy life's pleasures.

The steward brought me a cup of coffee and offered me a pastry. It was golden, light, filled with cheese. I didn't have to worry about this food. I took a sip of coffee, inhaling its rich aroma, and leaned back in my seat.

I was on my way home.

chapter 12

Graduation

I disembarked the Air France airliner at LAX, anticipating the worst as I prepared to pass through customs. My last two airport security experiences had left me shaky. It surprised me when I handed the customs officer—a woman— my declaration form, paid my sixty-five dollars in duty, and immediately gained entry into the United States without fuss, ado, or a prolonged interrogation.

A young gentleman, a porter, assisted me with my luggage. I ran to the exit gate. Nichole had promised to be here to meet me. As I rounded the ramp, I reached into my pocket, pulled out my cotton kerchief, and stuck the white rag on my head.

When I walked into the main part of the terminal, Nichole scanned me. She didn't recognize me at first. Then her eyes widened in recognition, and she burst into laughter.

We hugged. *Now I knew I was home.*

One day soon after my return, Nichole rang me up on the phone. She initiated the conversation the way she usually does when she telephones.

"What are you doing?" she asked.

"Trying to figure it out," I said.

"Figure what out?" she asked.

"Life," I said.

"Like the rest of us know and it's a big secret we're not telling *you*. Well, keep working on it," she quipped. "Let me know when you get the answer, and I'll tell you if you've got it right."

Although we were bantering, our conversation summarized my overall response to the trip. I had found many useful, invaluable, and enlightening *pieces* in the Middle East. I had found the Key to

Power. Mysteries had been revealed. But despite my discoveries, something was still out of sight, out of grasp, and just out of reach.

I hadn't yet found *the* missing piece.

One of the first things I did when I returned home was to lighten my hair. My friend and hairdresser, Angelo, who had darkened my hair for the trip, now began to turn me blonde. He insisted it was an important part of my life, my work, and this book. He said my *auric* field was lightening, and it would help to have my hair lighter too, for a while. I didn't argue. Angelo had an uncanny ability to synchronize my hair with my life. My hair and clothing had now become almost costumes—important, but still costumes. For some reason, it felt natural to go lighter and become a blonde.

It took a month to heal my stomach from the effects of drinking the Moroccan milk. I also discovered that what demanded healing wasn't just the current effects of drinking milk processed differently than my digestive track could assimilate. The entire excursion had spurred and activated a much deeper healing process. Whether I consciously desired to go through this intense and often surprising agendum was irrelevant. The wheels had been set in motion. There was no turning back.

The crescent moon and star continued to appear—on signs, on posters, on jewelry, and occasionally in the early morning sky. I still didn't understand what this sign meant. But I knew it was an important picture—a sacred symbol that spoke directly to my heart and mind.

Old treasured values resurfaced and reappeared. *Love thy God with all thy heart, and soul, and mind. Honor the Sabbath—whatever day your heart says the Sabbath is. Do not covet. Love thy neighbor. And, borrowing Tommy Boy's favorite line, **for the love of God** remember to love yourself.*

It had been one thing to see the forces of the universe at work when traveling through the western United States. It had been another to see the universe dance for me in terrorist-infested nations halfway across the globe.

This trip had revitalized my faith in God, in the universe, and in myself.

It would take months for me to integrate what I had learned and understand the importance of what I had seen. I hadn't just collected a few trinkets of wisdom to keep in a treasure chest and take out and examine at my leisure. I had been undeniably changed by what I had seen and experienced, by all that had taken place.

I was being transformed.

I had been through an initiation. It had included a review and demonstration of key lessons of the past. But this obstacle course I had stumbled through had also revealed important clues about how the energy at this new level would work.

As we ground or sped toward it—depending on the mood of the day—we had all embarked upon a new time.

The millennium had arrived.

The word "mystery" grew in importance. Lessons and insights began to unfold with the subtle intrigue of a Raymond Chandler mystery novel plot. Slowly, I began to trust and sometimes play with this energy, almost the way I would play a parlor game. Trying to know too much too soon or before it was time created a tormented inner struggle. Resistance led nowhere worth going. It only caused pain.

"Integrity" became a key word, too. Anything could happen at this new level, but it wasn't a time of anything goes. Manipulation, hustles, cutting corners, denials, sliding by, less-than-honorable intentions, and little white lies immediately came to light. The energy of this new time was alive, vibrant, intuitive bordering on psychic. It demanded the truth.

Hurrying and rushing no longer worked as well—or at all. An anxiety-ridden pace slowed me down. I'd get a running start, then run smack into a wall. The new timing that prevailed was persistent and not necessarily my own. I had to learn to take the time I needed.

Details became critical at this heightened, accelerated but microscopic pace. While the movement sometimes felt way too slow, this new energy whirled through me, bringing change *and* healing at top speed—if I took my time and revered each piece.

Although at times I got weary of monitoring everything I ate and did, I began to pay even closer attention to what was toxic to me. We need to be at our strongest and best for the powerful creative forces that have been unleashed in the world to work.

One month after I returned home, when my stomach began to heal, I took a trip to the redwood forest at Big Sur. It was supposed to be a quiet weekend getaway.

That's when I had the unsettling dream about an alchemist (one who has magical powers to transform dross into gold) who had gotten reckless with his ax. In the alchemist's eagerness to transform his life experiences into gold, he had mistakenly hacked away at himself. His alchemy had gone bad. Now, in the dream, he hid in bed under sheets and a quilt. In his desire to work his wizardry, he had cut himself up so badly there was almost nothing left. He felt so ashamed he wanted no one to see what he had done.

The dream left me unnerved. Recently I had bought an ax so I could chop wood for my outdoor stove. Maybe the dream is just a nightmare, brought on by eating too late in the day, I thought. Or perhaps the dream is an admonition to be careful with my new ax.

I tried to dismiss the dream as irrelevant, but this dream wouldn't let me loose.

Slowly it began to unravel. The hair stood up on my arms when I understood and got it right. After traveling halfway around the world, I finally found the missing piece.

All along, it had been me.

In the name of God, spiritual growth, and trying to be nice and do things right—I had given away, as Janis Joplin wails about in her song, a lot of pieces of my heart.

I had handed over my esteem to those who hadn't been able to love me, either because it wasn't their destiny or desire. "Here, take it," I had said. "You must be right. There's something wrong with me." I had never learned the rules, the rules for how to be loved. I had given away my power to love, to be loved, and most of all, to love myself.

To those who had betrayed me, I had given the best pieces of my heart and soul. I had given them my hope, my ability to be fulfilled, and my compassion for myself. I had given up what I knew to be my truth. I had foregone my right to be free from lies and deception. Instead I had learned to betray myself. I had given so much and settled for so little in return. It was a deadly, spirit-killing game. These were the most precious pieces of my heart. God, it was time to get them back.

It was time to really love myself.

To those who said they knew better and more about what was right for my life, I had systematically relinquished my power. I had given up my ability to think and to feel and to stumble around and find my own path. I had given away so much of my power my light had almost gone out. I needed to remember that each of us is valuable and has something important to contribute to the world. And *my* answers were in *me*.

I had given away my freedom to a lot of boxes and traps—from money, to sick love, to all the "have-to's," " should's," and "shouldn't's" floating around in society and embedded in my head. I had clipped my own wings and sat locked in a cage feeling bitter, powerless, and trapped. I didn't have to stay there. I knew how to fly.

To the dark forces of grief that had weakened my heart, I had given my ability to experience joy. I had begun to believe that life was only about loss. I thought it was supposed to hurt and be hard. What were those words I used to believe? "Everything works out for good. There is a Plan. I can really and truly trust God."

I had given my voice to those who would benefit by my silence. So many words were stuck in my throat I could barely speak anymore. I had forgotten how to scream in rage, shout for joy, say "Get away" or "Come close." I had learned to expertly acquiesce. I had forgotten how important my words are. It was time to start speaking my piece.

I had learned to overlook way too much. I had lost my stick. We each have so much emotional and spiritual power. I needed to remember what was important not just to others, but to me. It helps everyone when we tell people to stop.

To those people who hadn't protected me, I had given my right to feel safe. I had forgotten how to trust life and myself, to feel secure and out of harm's way. I thought I had to feel frightened and on guard. It was time to get back my peace. I knew how to protect myself.

To those who hadn't wanted me—at least not the way we want to be wanted—I had given my right to be here. Maybe they hadn't chosen me, but I could choose myself. All of us who are here now have chosen to be here for this transformational time. *We are the chosen ones.*

To all my dreams that had been shattered and lost, I had given my ability to dream again. I didn't think there was anywhere new left to go. I didn't think there was much left that merited hope. An important part of me had died. I had forgotten how to wish. I thought dreams were stupid and just for the weak, not for people who had sense. I didn't think there were any prizes left, at least not in this world, not for me. It was time to get back my sense of wonder and awe. I wanted to throw pennies in the fountain again and make a wish upon a star.

Now that I knew what was missing, I wanted all these pieces back.

We don't have to settle for one iota less than we deserve, and our birthright is to be whole, complete, and intact. What we need to know is not how wrong we've been but how wonderful our souls and lives are.

Soon after my discovery at Big Sur, Nichole tele-phoned me at the lodge. She had news she was excited to tell me. She couldn't wait until I arrived home.

"Master Huang is coming back to town," she said. "It's time for you to get your Tao."

I had been waiting for this for a long, long time.

The initiation was complete. I had just passed the test.

The final message of the trip was about to be-come clear: *If you feel like life has become an obstacle course, don't lose faith. If all the old doors appear to be closing, a new door will soon open wide. This one will be the gateway to a new dimension of life.*

At 3:00 P.M. on March 3, 1996, I walked through the front doors of the Venice Holy House, in Venice Beach, California. The front yard was a peaceful landscape, a Zen garden. The house smelled intoxi-catingly rich with all the delicious vegetarian dishes that had been cooked and spread about in prepara-tion for a feast.

Nichole accompanied me. Throughout the after-noon, she stayed by my side. She had been through this before. She would be an escort, a guide, and give testimony as to my character when the ceremony began.

At 3:30 P.M. that day, my full name including my maiden name—Melody Lynn Vaillancourt Beattie—

was entered in the Book of Life. I was told this recording was a formality; it had been there all along. After carefully writing down the spelling of my name, the man taking the information, Master Huang's assistant, told me to proceed to the back room of the Holy House.

The ceremony was about to begin.

First the men, then the women, were called by name to come to the front of the room. When my name was called, I tenuously took a position in the back row of the women kneeling before the altar. The woman assisting Master Huang, a Chinese woman who spoke no English, motioned for me to trade places with someone in the front. She told me to sit by the incense pot—the same position that she had directed Nichole to four months earlier.

I stumbled through the repetitive liturgy—imitating the sounds and repeating the Chinese words the best I could. Master Huang then approached each of us, one at a time. He put his hand on my head and asked if I was ready to take this step. I said I was. He then pronounced that I had officially received my Tao.

After spending a moment with each of us in the group, Master Huang told us that just as the candles on the altar burned brightly, so now did the light within each of us. Our karma was ended.

Reincarnation would cease. We had reached and achieved the state the ancients called enlightenment.

He told us to return to our chairs.

Carefully, so as to be understood with his Chinese accent, Master Huang gave us the Three Treasures. He explained them carefully, tracing the Treasures to their biblical origins. Then we each took a vow of secrecy.

The Treasures were not ours to reveal.

Master Huang told us it was time to smile. We had now received the keys to the Kingdom of Heaven—*to Paradise*—in the afterlife *and* in this world.

This is what he said next:

"For thousands of years on this planet, enlightenment has been available to only a few. Throughout the history of man, there has usually been only one enlightened being on the earth at a time. Now that the millennium is here, enlightenment will be given to the masses.

"It's a gift of the times. And a sign of the times.

"Enlightenment is now available to all.

"One at a time, across the globe, the lights will be turned on until the brilliance of this planet glows."

When I arrived home that day, I knew I had just taken part in an important and sacred event, but I was still uncertain about exactly what had transpired.

Master Huang's words stuck in my mind. "You don't have to worry or ask questions. Each person will be shown what to do."

I went to bed early that evening. I was exhausted, but tired in a good way. As I began to drift into sleep, the Santa Anas started blowing again. The winds encircled the house like a vortex, the same as they had before this trip began. They blew so hard the windows shook, the doors rattled, and the bird began to squawk.

The next morning, first thing, I checked outside. Those winds had taken my garbage can again.

"That's it," I said. "I'm done. This is the last time this will ever take place."

I trudged to the hardware store and bought a new can and a long, thin chain. I tied the chain around the trash can, securing it with several tight knots, then nailed it to the mailbox. "There," I said, pounding in the last nail. "That solves that once and for all."

I have never understood karma—not in the way a journalist needs to know. I'm not certain if it's cause and effect, unfinished business, or a spiritual consequence of something we can't remember but have nonetheless done. I'm not certain if karma is spiritual justice, the boomerang effect, or simply the way the universe brings itself into balance.

I still don't know, not in the way a journalist needs to know, if we live many lives or just one. I know that some people have experienced so much change it's been like having several lifetimes in one.

Maybe we just have to keep cycling through until we find all those missing pieces and finally take them back.

I don't know what it means to be karma-free, or if I really am. Maybe it means we can let the winds blow away all our old emotions and beliefs—*all the blocks to our power.* There's a higher road and a lower road to any place we want to go. The energy of these times brings the freedom to take that higher route.

Nichole pulled up in the drive just as I was testing the strength of the new chain that would secure my garbage can. It looked as if it would work.

"Did you figure it out yet?" she asked, following me down the stairs.

"Figure what out?" I said.

"Life. The book. Both," she said.

Now it was my turn to smile. "It's still a mystery to me."

O N WILL'S BIRTHDAY, he and Nichole came to the house. Something special was going on that weekend; I could feel it in the air. Nichole and Will went for a walk on the beach. It was the place they first had met.

When they returned to the house later that night, Nichole smiled—no, she *beamed*—and showed me her left hand. On it, she now wore a sparkling opal engagement ring. The children and I hugged and cried and talked and laughed. Then Nichole brought out Will's birthday cake.

He blew out all the candles except for one—a special candle that couldn't be extinguished no matter how hard he tried to blow out the flame.

"That candle is just like us," Nichole said, looking around the room. "No matter what we do to put it out, the flame keeps on burning bright."

THE END

Credits and Sources

Computer and Internet Resources

America Online Writer's Resources, including Compton's Encyclopedia, Grolier's Multimedia, and the Concise Columbia Library, provided instant access to facts on Algeria, terrorism, and the Middle East.

Compton's Interactive Encyclopedia, 1996, provided valuable data and facts about terrorism, Cairo, Egypt, Giza, the Great Pyramids, the Sahara Desert, Islam, Ramadan, the history of writing, language and art, the Seven Ancient Wonders of the World, Algiers, the Middle East, and Morocco.

World Wide Web, Elephants, Thomas Helton, 1996, "Tummy Rumble."

Government Agencies

Many United States government publications provided valuable facts and data on Algiers, Egypt, and Morocco.

The Embassy of the Democratic and Popular Republic of Algeria and the Egyptian Embassy were extremely helpful in preparing for this trip.

Miscellaneous

Brant Parker and Johnny Hart, creators of "The Wizard of Id."

Janis Joplin's Greatest Hits by Columbia provided the background music for writing this book.

A special thanks to the reference desks at the Ridgedale-Hennepin Area Library in Minnetonka, Minnesota, and the Southdale-Hennepin Area Library in Edina, Minnesota, for supplying factual data.

Virginia Slims commercial/ad was the source of the line used in the dedication.

Movies

Tombstone, Hollywood Pictures, written by Kevin Jarre, film by George P. Cosmatos, provided inspiration for the line on the "difference between a reckoning and revenge."

Tommy Boy, Paramount Pictures, A Lorne Michaels Production, film by Peter Segal, starring Chris Farley, for his tag line, "for the Love of God."

Publications

Algeria: A Country Study. Edited by Helen Chapin Metz. Library of Congress, Federal Research Division, 1994.

Arabian Nights. Adapted from Richard F. Burton's unexpurgated translation by Jack Zipes. New York: Penguin Books, 1991. Contains the tale of Scheherazade.

Bradshaw, John E. *Bradshaw on the Family*. Deerfield Beach, FL: Health Communications, 1988.

A Course in Miracles. Glen Ellen, CA: The Foundation for Inner Peace, 1975.

Critser, Greg. "Oh, How Happy We Will Be: Pills, Paradise, and the Profits of the Drug Companies." *Harper's Magazine*, vol. 292, no. 1753 (June 1996).

Eadie, Betty J., with Curtis Taylor. *Embraced by the Light*. Placerville, CA: Gold Leaf Press, 1992.

Holy Bible, Authorized or King James Version. World Bible Publishers, 1989.

Jochmans, Joseph. "How Old Are the Pyramids?" *Atlantis Rising*, no. 8, Livingston, MT.

Lamott, Anne. *Bird by Bird*. Garden City, NY: Doubleday, Anchor Books, 1995. This book, a *must read* for any writer, aspiring or published, provided me with professional support, wisdom, and the particular impetus for my definition of self-love. The line referred to is one where Anne writes that she believes "nothing is the opposite of love."

New World Translation of the Holy Scriptures. Brooklyn, NY: Watchtower Bible and Tract Society of New York, 1961, 1981, 1984.

Peck, M. Scott. *The Road Less Traveled.* New York: Simon & Schuster, Touchstone, 1978.

Simon, Jeffrey D. *The Terrorist Trap: America's Experience with Terrorism.* Bloomington and Indianapolis, IN: Indiana University Press, 1994.

Sun Tzu. *The Art of War.* Translated by Thomas Cleary. Boston and London: Shambhala, 1988.

Williamson, Marianne. *A Return to Love.* New York: HarperCollins, 1992.

Zwingle, Erla. "Morocco: North Africa's Timeless Mosaic." *National Geographic,* Oct. 1996, vol. 190.

And...

A thank you and acknowledgment to:

Gregg Baxter, for writing the beautiful letter.

Jen Bush, for discovering with Nichole the marvelous pigs and vampires theory.

Angelo DiBiase, my friend and hairdresser, for costuming me.

Michael Fowler, my Aikido *sensei,* from the War and Peace Dojo, Santa Monica, CA, for patiently teaching me Aikido and providing a helpful brochure from which I derived my definition and description of Aikido.

Marjorie Campbell-Perfilio, for telling me the beautiful stories about herself and about Johann Strauss, and for her encouragement along the way.

And her son, Christopher Perfilio, for bringing Marjorie and me together.

Ann Poe, for helping me solve a few of this book's mysteries.

Michael Powers, Los Angeles, California, for the author photograph.

Charlie Raun, for the delightful story of the "Don't Help" hand.